Contents

GW00505802

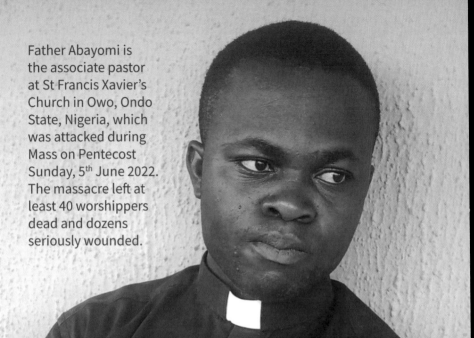

Father Abayomi is the associate pastor at St Francis Xavier's Church in Owo, Ondo State, Nigeria, which was attacked during Mass on Pentecost Sunday, 5th June 2022. The massacre left at least 40 worshippers dead and dozens seriously wounded.

I was still saying Mass when I heard the explosions. I was on the sanctuary, putting incense in the thurible, preparing for the procession outside the church, when I heard two loud noises and saw my panicked parishioners running in different directions. Someone ran to me and shouted: "Father, unknown gunmen!"

I don't know how many of them there were – some say six, others say four – but I do know they were organised. Some of the attackers disguised themselves as parishioners and worshipped with us during Mass, knowing the whole time they intended to kill us.

As bullets filled the air, I thought only of how to save my parishioners. Some of them managed to lock the entrance door and I urged people to move into the sacristy. Once in the inner part of the sacristy, I could not move: children surrounded me, and adults clung to me. I shielded them just as a hen shields her chicks.

My flock, especially the children, cried out: "Father, please save us – Father, pray!" I told them not to worry, as God would do something. There were three or four more explosions, one after the other inside the Church and there was sporadic shooting of guns by the attackers. It was a well-planned attack that lasted about 20-25 minutes.

Once the message came that the attackers had gone, we left the sacristy. Dead bodies were strewn across the church and there were many injured. My spirit was deeply troubled. With the help of parishioners who could drive, we immediately began to take our injured brothers and sisters to St Louis Hospital and the Federal Medical Centre. Since then, I have visited the wounded, praying with them, administering the Sacrament of the Sick and encouraging them to keep hope alive.

The world has turned away from Nigeria. A genocide is taking place, but no one cares. Nearby security personnel and police failed to come to our rescue, even though the attack lasted at least 20 minutes.

Aid to the Church in Need (ACN)'s publication of *Persecuted and Forgotten? A Report on Christians oppressed for their Faith 2020–22* is vitally important as it highlights the dire threats facing believers. It is not just Christians in Nigeria who suffer, but those in Pakistan, China, India and many other places.

Christians are killed all across Africa, their churches attacked and villages razed to the ground. In Pakistan, they are unjustly detained on spurious charges of blasphemy. Underage Christian girls are kidnapped, raped, forced to convert and marry middle-aged men in countries such as Egypt, Mozambique and Pakistan. In China and North Korea, totalitarian governments crush the faithful underfoot, monitoring their every move. And, as this report shows, the list of abuses goes on.

The suffering Church needs people to speak out for us. For the killing to stop, more organisations like ACN need to proclaim the truth of what is happening to Christians all over the world. If not, we will always remain persecuted and forgotten.

Main Findings

"My God, it is hard to be chained and to receive blows, but I live this moment as you present it to me… And, in spite of everything, I would not want any of [my captors] to be harmed."[1]

These are the words of Sister Gloria Cecilia Narváez, speaking to Aid to the Church in Need in January 2022, three months after her release from captivity in Mali, west Africa. She was held by Islamist militants for four-and-a-half years, during which time the Franciscan Sister was repeatedly physically and psychologically tortured. Sister Gloria made clear that her Christian faith was the source of the animus against her. She described how her captors became enraged when she prayed. On one occasion, when a jihadist leader found her praying, he struck her saying: "Let's see if that God gets you out of here." Sister Gloria continued: "He spoke to me using very strong, ugly words… My soul shuddered at what this person was saying, while the other guards laughed out loud at the insults."[2]

Sister Gloria's shocking account highlights the suffering inflicted on people whose only crime is their Christian faith. *Persecuted and Forgotten?* provides first-hand testimony; case studies; country, regional and global analysis on the extent to which Christians are targeted around the world. In the run-up to the period under review, human rights violations against Christians deteriorated sharply, with the Pew Research Center's figures for 2019 showing that Christians were harassed in more countries than any other faith group.[3] There was also a sudden increase in violations against Christians – up from 145 countries in 2018 to 153 a year later.[4] Open Doors' 2022 World Watch List reported "seismic changes in the persecution landscape"[5] for Christians. For the first time in the survey's 29-year history, all worst-offending 50 countries scored "high" persecution levels.[6]

Evidence collected for this edition of *Persecuted and Forgotten?* suggested that in many countries the situation for Christians continued to decline in the period under review which ran from October 2020 to September 2022. By no means exhaustive, this eighth edition of the report examines the situation in 24 countries where religious freedom violations against Christians are of particular concern. This provides an insight into the nature and severity of human rights abuses suffered by Christians and, in many cases, other minorities.

The key findings of *Persecuted and Forgotten?* 2020–22 are:

- In 75 percent of countries surveyed, the oppression or persecution of Christians increased.

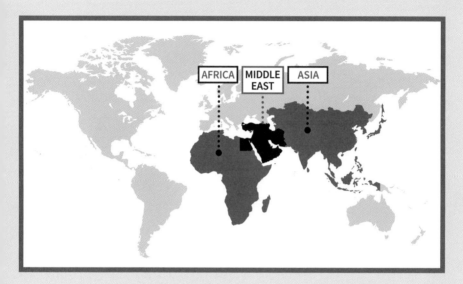

- In Africa, the situation of Christians worsened in all countries reviewed[7] amid evidence of a sharp increase in genocidal violence from militant non-state actors, including jihadists.

- In the Middle East, continuing migration deepened the crisis threatening the survival of three of the world's oldest and most important Christian communities located in Iraq, Syria and Palestine.

- In Asia, state-authoritarianism has been the critical factor causing worsening oppression against Christians in Burma (Myanmar), China, Vietnam and elsewhere. At its worst, freedom of religion and conscience is being strangulated, as in North Korea.

  Elsewhere in Asia, religious nationalism has caused increasing persecution against Christians in Afghanistan, India, Pakistan and elsewhere.

Regional analysis

Africa

Mali
WORSE
Radical extremist groups have now seized central areas of the country, further adding to instability.

Sudan
WORSE
A military coup in October 2021 has plunged Christians back into uncertainty, with persecution on the rise.

Eritrea
WORSE
The situation in Eritrea itself remains the same, but Eritrean troops were implicated in atrocities against Christians in Tigray.

Nigeria
WORSE
The number of attacks and killings has sharply risen, with more than 7,600 Christians killed during the period under review.

Ethiopia
WORSE
The conflict in the Tigray region has led to increased attacks against Christians, including massacres and the destruction of historic monasteries.

Mozambique
WORSE
Islamist attacks by Al-Shabab have led to the displacement of more than 800,000 and the death of more than 4,000.

Christians across the continent face the threat of rising Islamist extremism. Groups like Nigeria's Boko Haram and Islamic State West Africa Province (ISWAP) still try to establish caliphates in the Sahel region, each with its own wali (governor) and governing structure. Taking a hard-line Salafi-jihadist stance, the Islamic State in the Greater Sahara (ISGS) banned music and parties, and heavily regulated social events like weddings.[8] In June 2021, ISGS fighters executed five Christian civilians seized at a roadblock between Gao, Mali, and Niamey, Niger.[9] In Mozambique, Al-Shabab stepped up its terror campaign, killing Christians, attacking Christian villages and burning down churches. The group is affiliated to Daesh (ISIS), which claimed responsibility for the March 2021 attack on Palma, north-east Mozambique.[10]

Jihadism is one reason why **Nigeria teeters on the brink of becoming a failed state,** with kidnappings, priests killed and deadly attacks on churches becoming increasingly regular. According to one analysis, between January 2021 and June 2022, more than 7,600 Christians were killed.[11] Controversy arose in November 2021 when the United States government removed Nigeria from its list of "Countries of Particular Concern" in regard to religious freedom. Rev'd Samson Ayokunle, president of the Christian Association of Nigeria, hit back, saying there was a militant extremist agenda to "wipe away Christianity".[12] Indeed, in 2020 extremists exploited coronavirus restrictions to attack Christian settlements. A letter from UK Parliamentarians and charities warned the British government that militant members of the Fulani herder community had been "taking advantage of COVID-19 lockdowns to intensify attacks on villages" in Nigeria's Middle Belt.[13] Two major incidents of Christian persecution in Nigeria made international news. First was the stoning to death, and setting alight, of Deborah Samuel, a 25-year-old Christian, in May 2022, after she shared "blasphemous" messages on WhatsApp. Second was the deadly attack on St Francis Xavier's Church, Owo, Ondo State, during Mass on Pentecost Sunday, killing at least 40.

Extremist groups are not the only problem on the continent and **state actions have hit Africa's Christians detrimentally**. With the removal of President Omar Al-Bashir in April 2019 ending a period of increasing Islamism, Christians in Sudan were waiting to see how the new government would act after the 2021 military coup. Early signs were not encouraging, with Church leaders detained and a couple charged with "adultery" because the husband converted to Christianity. On 24th June 2022, four men were arrested on grounds of apostasy, although they were later released. According to reports, they were subjected to degrading and inhuman treatment.[14]

In-country sources suggested both Eritrean and Ethiopian troops attacked clergy and church buildings in Ethiopia's Tigray region. Eritrean troops stand accused of a campaign of ethnically motivated "cultural cleansing", reportedly participating in massacres of Ethiopian Christians, such as the one at Aksum, as well as destroying ancient monasteries and church buildings. In May 2021, Patriarch Mathias, the head of the Ethiopian Orthodox Tewahedo Church, said the Ethiopian government, with the help of Eritrean forces, "want to destroy the people of Tigray" – asking why Ethiopia wanted to "declare genocide on the people of Tigray".[15] That same month, ACN was told that nuns had been raped as part of the attack on Tigray.[16]

Middle East

Paradoxically, there are signs that in parts of the Middle East Christians are in a worse situation than during the Daesh (ISIS) occupation. Evidence came to light showing the threat to the survival of some of the world's oldest Christian communities had significantly deepened. The decline is most marked in Syria where, within a decade, Christians have plummeted from 1.5 million (10 percent of the population) in 2011, before the war began, to perhaps 300,000 (less than two percent of the population). In the aftermath of the 4th August 2020 Beirut explosions, where the greatest impact was felt in the Christian quarter, Lebanon's Church leaders questioned the community's long-term survival. In Iraq, where the rate of exodus is much slower, the community is down from perhaps 300,000 before the 2014 Daesh invasion, to as few as 150,000 in Spring 2022. ACN research showed that in parts of Iraq where Christians had been a strong minority, such as the capital Baghdad, the community was a shadow of itself, with churches struggling to stay open. However, of the seven Middle East countries in this review, Iraq was the only one to see an improvement. A comprehensive post-Daesh stabilisation programme involving the rebuilding of Christian towns and villages, homes, schools, churches and other public facilities was crowned by the long-awaited Papal visit of March 2021.

And yet in Iraq, as in so many other Middle East countries, the Christian community feels the danger posed by the underlying menace of jihadist groups. Continuing Islamist violence, for example in northern Syria, showed that even denouncement of extremism by senior Islamic leaders was apparently making little impact on the ground. Indeed, the extremist threat persisted across the region. **More than five years on from the military defeat of Daesh, the threat of a full-scale resurgence has by no means disappeared. A revival of jihadism has the potential to deliver**

Israel/Palestine
NO CHANGE
Christians still attacked by radical groups. Authorities accused of sometimes failing to support communities.

Turkey
SLIGHTLY WORSE
Ongoing tensions with state exacerbated by projects to re-Islamise historic Christian sites.

Iraq
SLIGHTLY BETTER
2021 Papal visit celebrated rebuilding of decimated Christian communities after genocide, but growth limited by state oppression and militant groups.

Iran
NO CHANGE
Christians continue to live under extreme oppression, with proselytising by non-Muslims punishable by death.

Qatar
SLIGHTLY WORSE
Despite improvements, including removing some anti-Christian references in school text books, there has been a sharp rise in reports of intolerance.

Egypt
NO CHANGE
Increased government support offset by continuing attacks, abductions of women and other problems.

Syria
SLIGHTLY WORSE
Much-reduced Christian communities beset by extreme malnutrition, Islamist oppression and attacks on some Christian-majority towns and villages.

Saudi Arabia
SLIGHTLY WORSE
Extremist violence including 2020 attack on a rare Christian cemetery. Ongoing bans on Christian places of worship and public display of crosses, Bibles, etc.

a knock-out blow for Christianity in its ancient heartland. This is not only because the numbers of Christians are now so low but also because their confidence is so fragile; they may have made it through times of genocide but, in the absence of security, the draw of migration is – for many of them – all but irresistible. That desire to leave is magnified in a cultural setting which remains antipathetic to Christians. Treated as second-class citizens, discriminated against at school and in the workplace, poor pay or joblessness trigger many to seek a life outside the country.

This existential threat extends to parts of Israel/Palestine. Nearly 75 years on from the creation of the state of Israel, Christians in the West Bank have declined from 18 percent to less than one percent today. Again, militants are a major concern. Groups such as Hamas were seen as factors driving migration in the West Bank. Although the overall number of Christians in Israel is growing – increasing by 1.4 percent in 2021 – ongoing attacks by fringe groups led Church leaders to speak of "a systematic attempt to drive the Christian community out of Jerusalem and other parts of the Holy Land".

In Saudi Arabia and elsewhere, there is a lack of political will to uphold constitutional commitments to religious freedom. The adherence to *Shari'a* law trumps statutory requirements regarding rights for all. **In such places, Christians are a silent, unseen minority – and there is little sign of change on the horizon.** Such countries in the region still enforce a ban on church-building, the public display of crosses and other Christian symbols, and the import of Bibles and other Christian texts.

Asia

In varying degrees, from tightening constraints in Vietnam to an almost total ban in North Korea, **state authoritarianism restricts – or even strangulates – believers' ability to worship freely.** While government attempts to regulate religious believers' practice of their faith are not unique to the region, they are characteristic of a number of countries in Asia. China continues to harass and attempt to control Christians and members of other religious groups that will not accept the official Communist Party line – making it unsurprising that in the Pew Forum's analysis of authorities' restrictions on religion it achieved the highest score of any nation

Afghanistan
WORSE
The rise of the Taliban has driven Christians underground – they live in fear of arrest, torture and execution.

China
WORSE
Authorities have increased pressure on Christians, with arrests, the forced closure of churches and new draconian legislation.

North Korea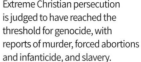
WORSE
Extreme Christian persecution is judged to have reached the threshold for genocide, with reports of murder, forced abortions and infanticide, and slavery.

Pakistan
WORSE
Increased reports of harassment, violence and gender-specific religious persecution. Growing threat of blasphemy allegations following 2021 legislation.

India
WORSE
More than 800 attacks on Christians over the period under review – a record high.

Maldives
NO CHANGE
Ongoing state oppression still forces Christians underground. Public display of Christian symbols, importing Bibles, etc. can result in imprisonment.

Vietnam
SLIGHTLY WORSE
As well as legal strictures, COVID-19 is now used by authorities as a pretext to restrict religious activity.

Sri Lanka
SLIGHTLY BETTER
Despite authorities still interfering with activities of Christian communities, no major incidents unlike previous period.

Burma (Myanmar)
WORSE
Following the military coup, the junta have renewed the targeting of churches and Christians.

state.[17] In Burma the army has renewed attacks on Christians, following a lull during Aung San Suu Kyi's administration. Despite the junta's previous promotion of Buddhism as the country's social norm, they are now targeting pagodas as well as churches, as they attack anyone perceived to oppose their 2021 coup.

Religio-nationalism has also played a significant role in repressing Christianity and other minority faith groups. Afghanistan is the worst offender, with the Taliban imposing a hard-line interpretation of *Shari'a* law on society. The Maldives also rigidly imposes Islam, even refusing citizenship for non-Muslims. In both countries it is nigh impossible to estimate the Christian population due to the assertion of the Islamic faith as the cultural norm. In India and Sri Lanka religio-nationalism is not as all-encompassing, but leads to ongoing attacks against Christians and other minorities. Hindutva and Sinhalese Buddhist nationalist groups have targeted Christians and their places of worship, and even police have been involved, arresting believers or stopping Church services. Political victories by religio-nationalist parties – Podujana Peramuna in Sri Lanka and Bharatiya Janata Party (BJP) in India – reinforce and encourage climates in which minorities are 'othered'. This 'othering' also occurs in Pakistan where Christians and members of other non-Muslim faiths can find themselves vulnerable within society and subject to increased risk of harassment, arrest and violence – which in some parts of the country frequently includes kidnapping and rape. Majoritarian religious beliefs are seen as the norm, fostering the perception that Pakistan is a monolithic Muslim state, in stark contrast with Jinnah's founding vision.

The advent of COVID-19 heralded problems facing Christians and other minorities across Asia, many of which started in early 2020 outside of the period under review. For example, in April 2020 ACN received reports that, in Pakistan, the local branch of the Saylani Welfare International Trust disregarded Christian homes during food distribution for poor families affected by the pandemic in Karachi's Korangi district.[18] This continued throughout the year with Islamic NGOs not helping non-Muslims where the aid had come from Zakat offerings – a form of religious almsgiving by Islamic adherents.[19] There is a tradition of non-Muslims being ineligible to receive Zakat, although this is a hotly discussed issue within contemporary Islam.[20] **State violations of religious liberty during**

the coronavirus pandemic ranged from the well-intentioned but draconian to the calculated and outright repressive. Sri Lanka fell into the former category: Christians and Muslims protested against the Ministry of Health's imposition of mandatory cremation for everyone who died, or was suspected of dying, from COVID-19 – a measure far exceeding WHO guidance and offending against both communities' traditional norm of burial. Meanwhile, Vietnam used the coronavirus as a pretext for repressive action against believers, and scapegoated at least one Christian community for the virus' spread in Hồ Chí Minh.

Conclusion

Indicators strongly suggested that over the period under review the persecution of Christians continued to worsen in core countries of concern. Religious nationalism and authoritarianism intensified problems for the faithful – including the Taliban's return to power in Afghanistan, which prompted Christians and other minorities to attempt a desperate scramble to escape. Systematic violence and a climate of control meant that in countries as diverse as North Korea, China, India and Burma, the oppression of Christians increased. At the same time, escalating violence – often aimed at driving Christians out – meant that the faithful suffered some of the world's most vicious campaigns of intimidation orchestrated by militant non-state actors. Of particular concern in this regard is Africa where extremism threatens previously strong Christian communities. In Nigeria and other countries this violence clearly passes the threshold of genocide.

Despite governments starting to recognise the importance of freedom of religion or belief, the evidence of this *Persecuted and Forgotten?* report shows there is a long way to go to ensure the liberty of Christians and other minorities around the world is protected. Part of the problem is a cultural misperception in the West that continues to deny that Christians remain the most widely persecuted faith group. Speaking out against this "political correctness", Chaldean Catholic Archbishop Bashar Warda of Erbil, northern Iraq, told Parliamentarians at a fringe meeting of the London FoRB Ministerial:

"There are still people being persecuted because of their faith… Yes, Christians are being persecuted."[21]

AFGHANISTAN

With the collapse of the government in Afghanistan, the withdrawal of US and NATO troops, and the rise to power of the Taliban in August 2021, the situation for Christians in Afghanistan became even worse than it was. In its 2022 World Watch List, Open Doors ranked Afghanistan as the most dangerous country in the world to be a Christian.[22] Due to the Taliban takeover, much of the small Christian population fled, estimated to be in the thousands. Those who remained live in fear of arrest, torture and execution. The Taliban have categorically denied the presence of Christians in Afghanistan, with spokesman Inamullah Samangani saying: "There are no Christians in Afghanistan. The Christian minority has never been known or registered here." [23]

Before the Taliban's takeover, Christians reported that public opinion, on social media and elsewhere, was hostile to Christian converts and the concept of Christian proselytisation.[24] They said they were pressurised, primarily by their families, to renounce Christianity and return to Islam.[25] They reported that individuals who had converted to Christianity,

or were studying to do so, received death threats, sometimes from family members.[26] Christians worshipped in small groups, often 10 or fewer, in private due to fears of societal pressure and discrimination.[27] However, following the takeover there were reports of Taliban raids on homes of converts to Christianity, even if they had already left the country or moved out.[28]

Despite initial statements suggesting that the Taliban would take a more liberal slant, it soon became apparent that those who did not adhere to their strict interpretation of Sunni Islam were in grave danger.[29] The Taliban's Ministry for the Propagation of Virtue and the Prevention of Vice, which cracks down on anything deemed un-Islamic, was reinstated.

Under the Taliban, a strict interpretation of *Shari'a* was instituted, including the death penalty for apostasy. The majority of the Christians in Afghanistan are converts.[30] Afghanistan has no long-established Christian traditions or denominations and all converts are considered apostates.[31] Not only do Christian converts face threats from the state but considerable pressure is exerted on them by their families and community, particularly in the rural areas. Conversion from Islam is seen as a threat to the Islamic identity of the country. The tight-knit nature of the Afghan family unit gives believers no privacy, with a high risk of discovery and intimidation from the wider community and the clan structure.[32] There is also the problem that Christianity is seen as Western, and therefore an enemy of Afghan culture, society and Islam.[33]

Under the previous government, some Christians felt sufficiently emboldened to list themselves as Christian on their identity cards. There were reports that the Taliban made it a priority to hunt down every single one of these 30 or so Christians who had declared their faith in this way.

International Christian Concern gave some examples of threats against Christians following the Taliban's takeover. One Christian man was

contacted by an extremist who told him he was going to kidnap his daughters and marry them off to members of the Taliban.[34] In another instance, the Taliban sent a letter to a Christian telling him his house now belonged to the Taliban.[35]

Christian women in Afghanistan face the threat of being sold into slavery or prostitution, being beaten, sexually abused, or being forced to marry a Muslim man to try and reconvert her.[36] Christian men, on the other hand, face pressure to show that they are good heads of a Muslim family, with "proper" beards, fasting and prayers five times a day. Their faith means they can face abuse, imprisonment, torture, sexual abuse and even death.[37] Both Christian men and women have to "pretend to be Muslim" to have any chance of peace. Many Christians turned off their phones and moved to undisclosed locations following the Taliban's takeover.[38]

Christians in Afghanistan also face danger from Islamic State: Khorasan Province (IS-K), which was responsible for the bombing of Kabul airport during the US evacuation in August 2021. IS-K threaten Christians with reprisals for conversion.[39] The Taliban considers IS-K an enemy.

August 2021 Following the Taliban's dramatic rise to power, Christians in Afghanistan reported receiving intimidating phone calls, with unknown people telling them: "We are coming for you". A Christian leader, who remained anonymous for security reasons, told International Christian Concern (ICC): "We are telling people to stay in their houses because going out now is too dangerous." He added: "Some known Christians are already receiving threatening phone calls."[40]

August 2021 Reports emerged that the Taliban were going door-to-door, killing Christians on the spot who refused to renounce their faith. Middle East Christian TV broadcaster SAT-7 reported that people were pulled off public transport and killed on the spot if they were found to be Christian, or ethnically "unpure". SAT-7's North America President Dr Rex Rogers said: "We're hearing from reliable sources that the Taliban demand people's phones, and if they find a downloaded Bible on your device, they will kill you immediately. It's incredibly dangerous right now for Afghans to have anything Christian on their phones. The Taliban have spies and informants everywhere."[41]

March 2022 The Taliban banned people from leaving the country as they continued their door-to-door "clearing operation", looking for Afghans with US relations and those, such as Christians, found to be violating the Taliban's stringent Islamist rule. A Taliban spokesman said: "I have to say clearly that persons who leave the country along with their families and have no excuse... We are preventing them."[42]

April 2022 A Christian in Afghanistan spoke out anonymously about the situation for the faithful in the country, saying that the Taliban are still hunting believers down. He said: "The situation here in Afghanistan for the Christians is not good," adding: "Believers are in grave danger. They are hunting the preachers and ministers door-to-door."[43]

April 2022 Reports emerged of the Taliban imprisoning and torturing a Christian because of his faith. Abdul spent months in captivity after trying to escape the country. A source close to Abdul's family said: "He reported that the first month, the Taliban torturers would bite him. The second month, they would put him in cold water at night and then leave him naked. The third month, they did not torture him, apparently wanting to sell him alive to his family without the evidence of torture. He does not leave the home where he is [now] staying."[44]

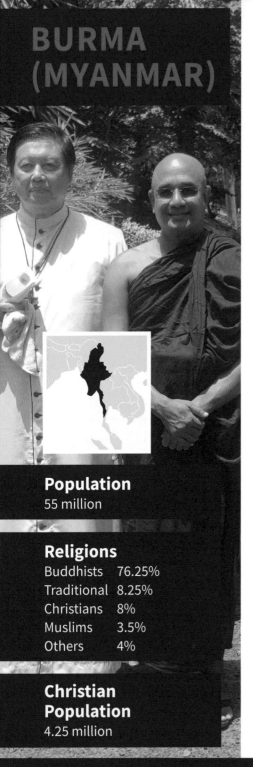

BURMA (MYANMAR)

Population
55 million

Religions
Buddhists   76.25%
Traditional   8.25%
Christians   8%
Muslims   3.5%
Others   4%

Christian Population
4.25 million

On 1st February 2021 the military's Commander-in-Chief, General Min Aung Hlaing, launched a *coup d'état*, seizing power and imprisoning members of the elected civilian government, including the head of government Aung San Suu Kyi, and key civil society activists. Several weeks of protests followed as tens of thousands of people took to the streets. There were reports of security forces using live ammunition as well as rubber bullets to crack down on protesters, leading to the deaths of more than 1,000 civilians.[45] Soldiers and police killed two activists after unarmed protesters sought sanctuary inside St Colomban's Cathedral, Myitkyina. On Sunday, 14th March – the same day that it was reported that up to 50 people were killed when government forces opened fire on unarmed protesters – Cardinal Charles Maung Bo, leader of the country's Catholics, made a fresh appeal for peace: "The killings must stop at once. So many have perished."[46]

Protests quickly spiralled into a *de facto* civil war. It was reported that, between February 2021 and the end of June 2022, the military had destroyed at least 132 Christian and Buddhist places of worship – despite vowing to protect Buddhism.[47] In Christian-majority Chin State, 66 churches

were destroyed during the same period. Often the army's reason, or at least pretext, for such attacks was that the churches were harbouring, or in some way connected with, resistance fighters. In Chin State in November 2021, St Nicholas' Catholic Church was burned down, along with the Presbyterian and Baptist churches and other buildings in Than Tlang, when the army accused locals of collaborating with rebels. The same month, the Baptist church in Ral Ti village was also torched.[48] In Kayah State, 20 churches were destroyed in the same period. One Kayah Christian leader said the regime deliberately targeted religious buildings outside of combat zones: "They are attacking the churches intentionally to suppress the spirit of Christian people by attacking their sacred churches."[49]

Targeted attacks were not new. Prior to the administration headed by Aung San Suu Kyi taking over, the ruling junta had implemented a campaign focused on bringing non-Burman ethnic tribes into obedience. This had a religious element as Christianity was more prevalent in the tribal areas – and even then there were reports of the army torching churches.[50] Kayah State, where 75 percent of the inhabitants are from ethnic minorities, has the highest percentage of Christians. There are over 90,000 Kayah Catholics, making up more than a quarter of the 355,000 inhabitants of the State, as well as a significant number of Baptists.[51]

Minority faith groups have also suffered because the military denied humanitarian aid organisations access to certain areas.[52] The local Church has provided humanitarian aid to the displaced who have taken refuge in churches and monasteries. For example, in Prang Hkung Dung parish, Banmaw Diocese, a Church-run camp for IDPs is caring for more than 3,000 people.[53]

March 2021 Sister Ann Nu Tawng knelt before armed police, begging them not to shoot young protestors sheltering in the compound of St Colomban's Cathedral in Myitkyina, the capital of Kachin State, on Monday 8th. Images of the Sister from the Congregation of St Francis Xavier in Myitkyina Diocese went around the world. But, as she knelt, police opened fire on the unarmed protestors behind her. Two were killed and seven others were injured. Sister Tawng previously made a similar plea for mercy on 28th February.[54]

May 2021 Four people were killed when government troops shelled Sacred Heart Church, just outside Loikaw, Kayah State where hundreds were seeking sanctuary. According to reports, more than 300 people sought refuge in the church after soldiers attacked the village seeking members of rebel groups.[55]

June 2021 Three Evangelical Pastors were arrested for having held an ecumenical prayer meeting for peace in Naw Mon, Kachin State on 3rd March. Pastors Koshan Singsar, Z Kaw Htinah and M Hawng Di were prosecuted under Article 505 (a & b) of the Myanmar Criminal Code which prohibits spreading terror, false news or subversion against the state.[56]

July-August 2021 Catholic priest Father Noel Hrang Tin Thang and catechist Clement Cung Hnin were released on 4th August, having been held by the rebel Chinland Defense Force (CDF) for just under a fortnight. CDF is a Chin State based militia group, founded following the military coup. The two men from Our Lady of the Rosary Church in Surkhua City were taken while getting medicine for parishioners, but were released after the Bishop of Hakha negotiated with rebels, signing a four-point promise, which included Fr Thang cutting off all contact with the Burmese army. The priest had previously interceded with a military general to prevent civilians being killed during fighting in Surkhua City. The Church is concerned that priests in contact with army or rebel groups may be seen as 'collaborators' by the other side.[57]

August 2021 Burmese soldiers occupied and profaned two churches in Chat village, Chin State on Tuesday 31st. At St John's Catholic Church soldiers opened the tabernacle, and threw consecrated hosts on the floor before trampling them. Cabinets and other furniture were destroyed, and similar damage occurred in Chat's Baptist Church.[58]

September 2021 Baptist Pastor Cung Biak Hum was shot dead while trying to extinguish fires started by the military in Thang Tlang, Chin State on Saturday 18th. According to Chin Baptist Convention, Pastor Hum's finger was cut off by soldiers to take his gold ring. His mobile phone and watch were also stolen.[59]

December 2021 The funeral took place of 35 Catholic civilians who were killed when their village of Mo So in Kayah State was attacked by junta forces on Friday 24th. After a delay of several days, military authorities allowed relatives to enter the village to claim the corpses. Among the dead were a three-year-old boy and a two-year-old girl who died with their parents. The funeral was led by catechists, as the military would not allow the parish priest into the area.[60]

February 2022 Soldiers arrested two Catholic priests – Father John Paul Lwel and Father John Bosco – transporting relief supplies to Le Htun village, Shan State. No reason was given for their arrest.[61]

March 2022 Burmese military targeted a church and convent on the outskirts of Demoso, Kayah State. The Church of Our Lady of Fatima in Saun Du La village suffered damage from an airstrike on Tuesday 8th March. A few days later, the convent of the Sisters of Reparation, where there is a respite home and hospital, was bombed.[62]

April 2022 Around 40 soldiers stormed Sacred Heart Cathedral, Mandalay during a Lenten service on Friday 8th and placed Archbishop Marco Win Tin, diocesan priests and cathedral staff under house arrest. Troops detained the congregation for around three hours. Soldiers remained in the cathedral throughout the night, saying they were searching for weapons. No arms were found.[63]

June 2022 The day after Our Lady, Queen of Peace Church in Doungankhar was shelled, Father Celso Ba Shwe, Apostolic Administrator of Loikaw Diocese in Kayah State, called for an end to attacks on places of worship. In the previous fortnight, Sacred Heart Church, Kantharyar village and St Joseph's, Demoso were also damaged.[64]

CHINA

Officially, Christians must be members of either the Three-Self Patriotic Movement for Protestants, or the Chinese Catholic Patriotic Association. There has been a long history of underground churches in China – both Catholic and Protestant – which are not permitted to hold public religious services or carry out other activities. Believers can be left facing imprisonment and fines.

Members of the Chinese Communist Party (CCP) and the armed forces are required to be atheists and are forbidden from engaging in religious practice.[65] The government has effectively banned under-18s from receiving religious education, or participating in religious activities, via the national law that prevents organisations or individuals from interfering with the state educational system for under-18s.[66]

In 2019, the CCP started a five-year plan to "sinicise" Christianity.[67] This called for "incorporating Chinese elements into church worship services, hymns and songs, clerical attire, and the architectural style of church buildings," while proposing to "retranslate the Bible or rewrite biblical commentaries."[68] In 2021, news emerged that the story of Jesus and the woman about to be stoned for adultery had been rewritten in an official ethics textbook. After waiting for her accusers to leave, Jesus stones the woman himself, saying, "I too am a sinner. But if the law could only be executed by men without blemish, the law would be dead."[69]

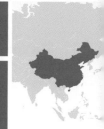

POPULATION
1.4 billion

CHRISTIAN POPULATION
104 million

RELIGIONS
Atheists or Agnostics 38.5% Ethnic or Folk religionists 35%
Buddhists 16.5% Christians 7.5% Muslims 1.75% Others 0.75%

The State Administration of Religious Affairs (SARA) issued regulations on "Administrative Measures for Religious Clergy", which took effect from 1st May 2021, requiring ministers of religion to pledge allegiance to the CCP and socialism. A database of "religious personnel" was also created. Authorities only issued "clergy cards" to Protestant or Catholic clergy who were members of the government-sanctioned churches. These cards certified that these persons were included in the national database of authorised clergy.[70]

The 2018 Regulations on Religious Affairs have also had a broad effect on religious practice in the country. They include fines for religious groups who do not seek approval to travel abroad for "religious training, conferences, pilgrimages, and other activities." The regulations also require that religious activity "must not harm national security" or support "religious extremism", without any definition of what constitutes "extremism". Measures to safeguard national unity and respond to ostensible extremism include the monitoring of individuals, institutions and groups. "Harm to national security" is punished by suspending groups and cancelling clerics' credentials.[71]

The historic agreement in 2018 between the Holy See and the People's Republic of China regarding the appointment of bishops was renewed for a further two years in 2020. The deal allows the CCP to have a say on the bishops that the Holy See appoints, while at the same time bringing all bishops in China in communion with Rome, ending illegitimate ordinations.[72] However, Bishop Simone Zhang Jianlin said that ordinations in Zhangjiakou Diocese were illegitimate and broke the terms of the agreement *(see May 2021).*[73]

Relations between the CCP and the Vatican became more strained following the arrest of 90-year-old Cardinal Joseph Zen Ze-kiun in May 2022, for his work with "612 Humanitarian Relief Fund", which gave financial support to pro-democracy protestors.[74] Cardinal Zen was later released on bail, and his trial was scheduled for late September. The situation for Hong Kong's Catholics worsened in the period under review, with shortages of Bibles due to government regulations[75] and warnings by the Vatican's unofficial representative in Hong Kong to prepare for CCP crackdowns *(see July 2022).*[76]

December 2020 Chinese government authorities restricted Christmas celebrations, designating only two acceptable forms of Christmas activity: either attending state-sanctioned churches, or celebrating Christmas at home.[77]

February 2021 The local authorities ordered the destruction of Sacred Heart Church in Yining, Xinjiang. Built in the year 2000, the Church holds all the required permits from the Administration for Religious Affairs – Yili district officials and Yining government authorities attended the inauguration, praising the construction. In 2018, as part of a "sinicisation" campaign, the Religious Affairs Office chiselled off four bas reliefs on the façade, removed the statues of Sts Peter and Paul, ripped off the cross adorning the cusp of the tympanum, and destroyed the two domes and bell towers for being "too showy". One believer said: "This is further confirmation that the country does not respect freedom of worship."[78]

May 2021 In Zhangjiakou, a diocese not recognised by the Holy See, priestly ordinations were carried out. Auxiliary Bishop Simone Zhang Jianlin of Xuanhua issued a statement arguing that Canon Law invalidated the ordinations, and that any sacraments celebrated by the new priests would be invalid.[79] Monsignor Gou Jincai, a formerly excommunicated bishop who was brought back into the Church by Pope Francis, acted contrary to the Code and Ecclesial Communion by not taking into account Vatican-recognised Bishop Agostino Cui Tai, who presides over Xuanhua Diocese which covers Zhangjiakou – Bishop Cui Tai has been in and out of police custody since 2007.[80]

May 2021 Bishop Joseph Zhang Weizhu, 10 priests, and 10 seminarians were arrested after organising an underground seminary for conscientious objectors who do not want to join the government-controlled Chinese Catholic Patriotic Association (CPA).[81] The seminarians were returned to their families, after being threatened with incarceration if they continued studying.[82] The priests were sent to Legal Education Centres, and then released. However, the whereabouts of Bishop Weizhu remain unknown.[83]

November 2021 A Christian couple who printed religious texts were sentenced to seven years in prison and fined approximately £29,240 for "illegal business operations". According to a Chinese human rights site, Chang Yuchun and Li Chenhui had their registered printing company seized by local authorities on 21st July 2020, after 210,000 copies of religious books were confiscated, with 24 titles later deemed "illegal publications".[84]

December 2021 An elder of Early Rain Covenant Church was arrested on Christmas Eve for "disturbing social order". Elder Li Yingqiang was planning to preach at an evangelical seminar over Zoom.[85]

February 2022 Independent house church leader Pastor Hao Zhiwei was sentenced to eight years on "fraud" charges in Ezhou, Hubei Province.[86] Pastor Hao, widowed with a young son, had been held in pre-trial detention since 31st July 2019. According to ChinaAid, he was detained for collecting offerings and preaching without state approval.[87]

May 2022 Cardinal Joseph Zen was arrested on 11th May 2022 by national security police, along with Margaret Ng Ngoi-yee, a former member of Hong Kong's Legislative Council, and Denise Ho Wan-sze, a singer.[88] They were charged with colluding with foreign forces. All were associated with the now defunct "612 Humanitarian Relief Fund" which helped protestors in financial need. If found guilty, they could face life imprisonment. Hong Kong police told the BBC that the group was suspected of appealing to foreign countries or organisations to impose sanctions on Hong Kong, thereby threatening China's national security.[89] Cardinal Zen was later released on bail. Matteo Bruni, the Director of the Holy See Press Office, said: "The Holy See has learned with concern the news of Cardinal Zen's arrest and is following the evolution of the situation with extreme attention."[90] On 25th May 2022, Cardinal Zen appeared in court in Hong Kong and pleaded not guilty.

July 2022 Archbishop Javier Herrera-Corona, the Vatican's unofficial representative in Hong Kong, warned the city's Catholic missions – numbering around 50 – that a crackdown was coming from the CCP.[91] He is reported to have said: "Change is coming, and you'd better be prepared", adding: "Hong Kong is not the great Catholic beachhead it was."

July 2022 The Catholic Diocese of Hong Kong announced on 25th July that there is a shortage of Bibles because printing houses on mainland China are unable, or unwilling, to print the Bibles. Friar Raymond Yeung, a member of the Diocese's Stadium Biblicum Franciscanum, told *Christian Times* that the printing house that used to print their Bibles stopped, as they had to get government permission to print.[92]

EGYPT

In 2022 the United States Commission on International Religious Freedom (USCIRF) recommended that the US government "Include Egypt on the US Department of State's Special Watch List for engaging in or tolerating severe violations of religious freedom".[93] Despite public support for the Christian community from the very highest levels of the Egyptian government, problems persist. Anti-Christian violence is ongoing, even if the period under review has seen a decline in the devastating extremist attacks by Daesh (ISIS)-affiliated groups. However, sporadic events such as the execution of Christian businessman Nabil Habashi Salama show they still pose a serious threat. Egypt has the largest Christian community in the Middle East and North Africa region. It is estimated that somewhere in excess of 90 percent of Christians belong to the Coptic Orthodox Church, with smaller communities of Coptic Catholics, Evangelicals, and other denominations. Their size may go some way to accounting for the hostility Christians encounter from some parts of the Islamic community.

Official permission for new churches used to take up to 30 years and required the President's personal approval, but the easing of legal restrictions and the granting of retroactive approval has been one of the most positive developments. In March 2022 President Abdel Fattah Al-Sisi

POPULATION
102 million

CHRISTIAN POPULATION
9.5 million

RELIGIONS
Muslims 90.25%   Christians 9.25%   Others 0.5%

signalled his support saying: "Where there is a mosque, there must also be a church. And if the church to be built will be attended by even only 100 people, it must be built anyway."[94] At the start of the period under review, in October 2020, the number of Christian places of worship that had been legalised had reached 1,738.[95] By April 2022 this had grown by 663 to 2,401.[96] There have been some commendable initiatives and in Minya Province – where 306 church buildings have been legalised since 2016 – Governor Oussama Al-Qadi set up a committee in 2021 to try to address all issues connected to church construction and renovation.[97] However, Minya Governorate's good intentions have not prevented demonstrations against official delays *(see January 2022)*, nor has governmental goodwill stopped social hostilities following churches' applications for legal registration *(see June 2022)*.

The abduction, forced conversion and marriage of Coptic Christian women continued throughout the period,[98] and could be increasing.[99] The scale of these crimes is under-reported, as victims are frequently reluctant to speak about these cases, which can involve rape and other degrading sexual abuse. Cases often only become known when family members take to social media, having failed to secure help from authorities.[100] There is evidence both of kidnapping gangs systematically targeting Coptic girls and of police officers having conspired to report them as missing rather than abducted.[101] Speaking in January 2022, Professor Michele Clark – who carried out first-hand research into this area – told ACN that there can be a genocidal element to these cases. Prof Clark said: "If a Christian woman is forced to convert or is forcibly married to a Muslim, it is impossible for her to return to her Christian faith... If the woman has children, these children will always remain Muslim... You are not only removing a single person from the group of Christians, but a mother and her progeny."[102]

Egypt's blasphemy laws continue to be a source of concern for human rights campaigners. Coptic Solidarity's Magdi Khalil, who has compiled a list of more than 100 cases mostly from the last decade, has suggested that "Egypt follows only Pakistan in the number and harsh implementation of blasphemy cases".[103] The vague terms of Egypt's laws on religious freedom have made it easier to discriminate against vulnerable minorities. In November 2020 a Christian man and a Muslim woman were arrested for Facebook posts under Article 98 (f) of Egypt's Penal Code, which criminalises insulting the three main monotheistic faiths *(see November 2020 below).*[104]

The ongoing use of reconciliation sessions to address attacks on Christians often leads to victims being forced to face their attacker, who is effectively spared anything but a token punishment. A reconciliation session was used after Coptic Christians' homes were torched in in Barsha village, Minya Governorate *(see November 2020)*. USCIRF condemned such meetings because they "regularly issue minimal penalties to assailants from the religious majority and often revictimise Christians by forcing them to admit culpability in attacks against them".[105]

November 2020 Christian teacher Youssef Hany from Ismailia was arrested for insulting Islam after he posted on Facebook. He was responding to a Muslim user who criticised President Macron and other French citizens for remarks made following the killing of the French teacher who showed the controversial cartoons of the Muslim Prophet Mohammed.[106]

November 2020 An elderly Coptic Christian woman was hospitalised for burns after her home was set on fire when a mob attacked a church, and Christian-owned houses and shops in Barsha village, Minya Governorate. The attacks followed an article considered offensive to Islam being posted on Facebook by a young Coptic man. 100 people were arrested, of which 35 were Copts – including Gerges Sameeh Zaki on whose Facebook page the piece appeared. He claimed his account had been hacked. A reconciliation session involving politicians, and religious and community leaders was held on 9th December 2020.[107]

March 2021 21-year-old university student Marian went missing from El-Marg, north-east Cairo Governorate. The married student was two months pregnant, and preparing to join her husband in the US, when she disappeared. He was sorting out her immigration papers at the time

the Christian woman vanished. In late July the man accused of abducting her posted photos on social media which appeared to show that he and Marian were a couple. There were speculations that these photos had been computer manipulated, and her family lobbied authorities to get involved in the case.[108]

April 2021 Islamic State: Sinai Province released a video of its members shooting dead 62-year-old Coptic Christian businessman Nabil Habashi Salama from Bir Al-Abd on the Sinai peninsula. Two young tribesmen who were also killed were accused of fighting alongside the military. His killers said: "As for you Christians of Egypt, this is the price you are paying for supporting the Egyptian army." Mr Habashi, who funded the building of St Mary's Church in Bir Al-Abd, was kidnapped in November 2020. Ransom negotiations continued until January 2021. Later that month the authorities asked his family to leave North Sinai. Forced to leave possessions behind, Mr Habashi's daughter Marina said: "Security forces left us on a road in the city of Ismailia with nothing." Marina has since received death threats on Facebook and demands that she convert to Islam. 11 members of Mr Habashi's family now occupy a two-bedroom flat.[109]

May 2021 St Macarius Monastery had part of its land seized forcibly by government officials on Sunday 30th following a rent disagreement. Despite a dispute between the monks and the government over the ownership of the land being settled, with the monks agreeing to pay rent in 2007, they defaulted on payments because of the COVID-19 pandemic.[110]

June-July 2021 Two 18-year-old girls who were abducted – Injy Rizk Farouq from Menoufia (June) and Marina Reda Zachari from Giza (July) – were returned to their parents. No details were released. It was speculated that, as in other cases, the families agreed to remain silent as part of the price for their daughters' return.[111]

September 2021 Christian man Gerges Sameeh Zaki, who was detained following the riots in Barsha in November, had his period of detention extended by 45 days by a ruling of Cairo's Counter Terrorism Court on Tuesday 7th. He was the only individual remanded in custody after January 2021. Despite insisting his Facebook account was hacked, he was accused of "joining a terrorist group, publishing fake news and disturbing public order, and using the internet with the intention to commit crimes."[112]

November 2021 Christian students at Al-Thawra School were beaten by teachers for wearing crosses. The headmaster of the school in Ezbat Beshri, Minya Governorate ordered pupils to remove any jewellery featuring a cross, and teachers and students later assaulted the Coptic Christians. It is common for Coptic Christians to wear crosses.[113]

January 2022 Security forces arrested at least nine Coptic Orthodox protestors demanding government approval for a new church. St Joseph and Abu Sefein (St Mercurius) Church in Ezbet Farag Allah village, Minya Governorate was gutted by fire in 2016. Some parishioners believe it was arson. Authorities granted permission to demolish the building but, more than five years on, had still not responded to an application to rebuild the church which serves the area's 800 Christians. The protestors from Ezbet Farag Allah were held in detention ahead of their trial on charges of terrorism and participating in a gathering that endangers public peace. Amnesty International, which called the terrorism charge "bogus", said that following their arrest, protestors were "interrogated while blindfolded and handcuffed, with no lawyers present" at a National Security Agency facility.[114]

April 2022 Coptic Orthodox priest Fr Arsanious Wadid died after being stabbed several times in the neck. The 56-year-old pastor of the Church of the Virgin Mary and St Paul in Alexandria's Moharam Bek district, died while being rushed to hospital on Thursday 7th. Police arrested his attacker, Nehru Tawfiq, soon afterwards. It is reported that he asked the priest for help before stabbing him. At trial it emerged that Tawfiq had been a member of the extremist Gamaa Islamiyah group that sought to establish a new caliphate in Egypt. He was found guilty on 18th May.[115]

April 2022 Coptic Christian woman Nevin Sobhi was repeatedly slapped and verbally abused by Ali Abu-Soaud, the Muslim owner of a chemist's shop, for going there without a head covering during Ramadan. The incident occurred on 21st April in Sabak Al-Ahad village, Monoufia Province, when the 30-year-old woman tried to buy medicine for her son who was with her. Nevin Sobhi experienced further problems when she went to the local police station to file a report. Arriving at 9pm, she did not get away until 3am. She was also pressured into signing a false report. A few days later she was made to attend a reconciliation session with her assailant.[116]

June 2022 Christian man Kyrillos Megally died after being pushed off his motorbike and repeatedly struck with a butcher's cleaver in Arab Mahdy village, Sohag Governorate. He died from his injuries on Tuesday 7th, after three days in intensive care. Abdullah Hosni was charged with the murder. He had previously been charged with assaulting two Coptic Christians.[117]

June 2022 Mobs rioted on Thursday 23rd, hurling rocks and setting light to buildings and vehicles after the Church of Michael the Archangel received formal legal recognition. Security officers failed to intervene as the attacks enveloped the Christian area around the church.[118]

July 2022 Christian man Joseph Israel and his son were hospitalised following a knife attack outside his off-licence in the Omranya District of Giza during the early hours of Thursday 28th. The Muslim attacker, Mr Mouhammad, was dragged off and beaten by some of the shopkeeper's Muslim neighbours.[119]

August 2022 Islamic State: Sinai Province were blamed for the fatal shootings of Coptic Christian man Salama Moussa Waheeb and his son Hany near Gelbana village in Al-Qantara Sharq, on Tuesday 30th. The men were working their farmland at the time.[120]

ERITREA

Population
5.4 million

Religions
Muslims   51.5%
Christians   47%
Agnostics   1%
Others   0.5%

**Christian
Population**
2.5 million

Since Eritrea's independence in 1993, President Isaias Afwerki and his political party, the Popular Front for Democracy and Justice (PFDJ), has ruled the country with an authoritarian approach.[121] The Eritrean constitution does guarantee freedom of speech, religion, conscience, and assembly, but in practice the government has restricted these rights. Proclamation No.73 of 1995 permits the government to exert complete control over religious activities in the country.[122]

There are only four permitted religions: the Eritrean Orthodox Tewahedo Church, Sunni Islam, the Catholic Church and the Evangelical Lutheran Church of Eritrea. Unregistered groups do not have the same privileges as registered groups, and members are often arrested and maltreated, being told they will only be released if they renounce their faith.[123]

It is quite common for members of unrecognised religious groups to report being arrested and detained with no explanation. For example, in April 2020, there were reports that the government arrested 15 Christians engaged in a worship service at a private home, and in June, a further 30 were arrested at a Christian wedding.[124] Reports suggest that there are 2,000 to 2,500 people detained in the Mai Serwa maximum-security prison, which is near the capital Asmara, 500 of whom are there because of their religion or belief.[125] According to Release International, in Eritrea, "citizens have a duty to report anything untoward happening in their community, turning ordinary neighbours into spies. There have been examples of people reporting their own family members for being Christians."[126]

It is a legal requirement in Eritrea that everyone aged between 18 and 50 has to serve in the military for 18 months, sometimes longer.[127] Eritrea imprisons those who refuse, including on religious grounds[128] – in order to be freed, they need to renounce their religious affiliation.

Yet, it is not just the unregistered churches that are suppressed by the Eritrean government. In May 2021, the government closed or nationalised nine schools, threatening to do so for 19 additional Church-run primary schools.[129] This followed a number of moves by the government before the reporting period. For example, in June 2019, the government seized three hospitals, two health centres and 16 clinics belonging to the Catholic Church, which served 170,000 people a year.[130] As a result, nuns were evicted with their belongings from the health centres where they worked and lived.[131] In September 2019, the government seized seven religious schools, four sponsored by the Catholic Church.[132] Catholic bishops said this move was motivated "by hatred against the faith".

The Eritrean government have also targeted the Eritrean Orthodox Tewahedo Church. In February 2022, Patriarch Abune Antonios died after being under house arrest for 15 years.[133] He was detained in 2007 and placed under house arrest, despite no charges being brought against him. He spoke out against government interference in Church affairs, refused to excommunicate 3,000 priests at the government's behest, and criticised the imprisonment of priests *(see February 2022)*.[134]

The US State Department has designated Eritrea a "country of particular concern" for persistent violations of religious freedom since 2004.[135]

October 2020 Five Christians were arrested after celebrating the release of 69 Christian prisoners. They stepped outside to pray and rejoice at the release of the prisoners who had been held in Mai Serwa

prison. The released prisoners were from Evangelical and Pentecostal backgrounds and had been imprisoned between four and 16 years. At least two were minors when their captivity began – one aged 16, the other 12.[136]

March 2021 35 Christians were arrested for conducting prayer meetings.[137] The army raided the meeting that was attended by 23 women in Asmara.[138] Another 12 were arrested in Assab, 660 miles south-east of Asmara, near the border with Djibouti.

May 2021 The Eritrean government targeted the Catholic Church, closing or nationalising nine schools and threatening to do so for 19 additional Church-run primary schools.[139] The Bishops in Eritrea spoke out against the decision, writing to the Eritrean Minister of Education, Mr Semere Reesom. They said: "The schools and clinics confiscated or closed, or about to be confiscated or closed, are the legitimate property of the Catholic Church, built, established and organised in the supreme and exclusive interest of serving our people."[140]

July 2021 Two pastors were arrested, with a third being placed under house arrest, in Asmara. All three were from the Full Gospel Church and were in their 70s. Pastor Girmay Araya and Pastor Samuel Okbamichael were taken at night and brought to the Wengel Mermera Central Criminal Investigation Interrogation Centre, which is part of Asmara's 2nd Police Station.[141]

September 2021 Authorities arrested 15 Christians in Asmara during raids on private houses, all of whom had been jailed for their beliefs previously. Some had served prison sentences of up to 16 years. Aged from their late 20s to their 60s, they were released in summer 2020 but rearrested after a list of Christian contacts was discovered. They were taken to Mai Serwa prison close to Asmara.[142]

February 2022 Patriarch Abune Antonios of the Eritrean Orthodox Tewahedo Chuch died after 15 years in government incarceration. Patriarch Antonios was 94 when he died at the Church residence in Asmara, where he was being kept under arrest. His body was taken to Abune Andreas monastery on 10th February and was buried at 9am. Large crowds gathered at his gravesite, many mourners had travelled long distances on foot. Abune Antonios became Patriarch of the Eritrean Orthodox Tewahedo Church in 2004 and was placed under house arrest in 2007, even though no formal charges were brought against him. He was punished for denying government requests to excommunicate 3,000 Church members, and spoke out about the imprisonment of Christians, including three Orthodox priests. Abune Antonios was kept in isolation for most of his time in detention, reportedly being denied medical care despite suffering from diabetes and high blood pressure.[143]

March 2022 29 Evangelical Christians were arrested after security forces raided a prayer meeting in a house in Asmara. 17 women and 12 men were taken to Mai Serwa prison. It is not known what prompted the raid by the security forces, although every residential area in Eritrea is reported to have a government spy living there.[144]

September 2022 Soldiers forcibly conscripted teenagers attending Mass at Medhanie Alem Church in Akrur village on Sunday 4th. Troops forced choir boys into military uniforms.[145]

ETHIOPIA

© Ismael Martínez Sánchez / ACN

In the period under review, the most significant development for the persecution of Christians has been the start of the civil war in the Tigray region of northern Ethiopia, which borders Eritrea. While the war was not religiously motivated, and it was not intended explicitly to stamp out the Christian presence in the region, a steady stream of reports have stated that Christians have been targeted and suffered extreme abuse.

The conflict started in November 2020, when Ethiopian Prime Minister Abiy Ahmed sent federal troops, supported by militia and army from Amhara, and troops from Eritrea, to fight the Tigray People's Liberation Front (TPLF), which he accused of holding illegitimate elections.[146]

Persistent reports say that Eritrean and Ethiopian troops have attacked priests, monks, nuns, and Church buildings, as a part of a campaign that has been described as "cultural cleansing", and even as "genocide" by Patriarch Mathias of the Ethiopian Orthodox Tewahedo Church.[147] There have also been accusations that TPLF have taken money, food and ancient manuscripts from churches, suggesting that the group is waging an "all-out war without giving due protection to religious sites and cultural properties".[148] Researchers at Belgium's Ghent University studying the conflict found in April 2021 that almost 2,000 people were killed in more than 150 massacres by soldiers, paramilitaries and insurgents in Tigray.[149]

POPULATION
113 million

CHRISTIAN POPULATION
68 million

RELIGIONS
Christians 59.75%   Muslims 34.5%
Ethno-religionists 5.5%   Others 0.25%

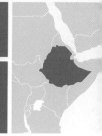

The nadir of the conflict was the reports, first from Belgian NGO European External Programmes with Africa (EEPA), and then corroborated by Amnesty International, BBC and many other major news organisations, of a massacre of reportedly up to 800 people at the Orthodox Maryam Tsiyon Church in Aksum.[150]

There have been persistent reports of massacres and rapes (including of nuns).[151] Eritrean troops have been accused of targeting churches and mosques as a policy of "cultural cleansing".[152] An anonymous source told ACN that "three parish priests have been threatened and beaten".[153]

In November 2021, Bishop Tesfaselassie Medhin of Adigrat called for an immediate end to the government's aerial bombardment of Tigray. Condemning the war as ethnic cleansing, he said the bombing was destroying lives, property, civilians and institutions in the region.[154] Bishop Medhin wrote an open letter in April 2022 on behalf of the Catholic Eparchy of Adigrat, again speaking out against the events in Tigray. He condemned the "genocidal massacres of civilians, rampant rape and gender related violence, looting and burning of property, homes, destruction of worship houses (churches, mosques)".[155]

The Ethiopian government have denied all the accusations against them, accusing the TPLF of waging a propaganda campaign. There has been a media blackout in the Tigray region since the beginning of the war, making verification of these events extremely difficult.

Cardinal Berhaneyesus Demerew Souraphiel, head of the Ethiopian Catholic Church, took a slightly more conciliatory approach to the conflict. He said: "The humanitarian situation in Tigray continues to worsen. The passage through the humanitarian corridors through which the United Nations, the government or other agencies try to bring food into the country, is sometimes blocked and we do not know for sure by whom".[156]

November 2020 Hundreds of people – including priests and other church elders – were killed in a series of attacks, culminating in a massacre at the Orthodox Maryam Tsiyon Church in Aksum (or Axsum), where the Ark of the Covenant is believed to be located.[157] A local source told ACN: "I heard there were 1,000 people in the church. It might be that more were injured and died later. 750 were killed for sure." They added: "In Aksum, there is the Ark of the Covenant. Maybe the people were there protecting the Ark and… they were taken outside and shot." Amnesty International verified the massacre in February 2021, after speaking to 41 survivors and witnesses to the mass killings. They said: "Eritrean troops fighting in Ethiopia's Tigray state systematically killed hundreds of unarmed civilians in the northern city of Aksum on 28-29th November, opening fire in the streets and conducting house-to-house raids in a massacre that may amount to a crime against humanity".[158]

February 2021 Ethiopia's most famous monastery – the Debre Damo Monastery in Tigray – was bombed and looted according to reports from the region. Eritrean soldiers allegedly scaled an 80-foot cliff to ransack manuscripts from the remains of the sixth-century monastery, prompting fears that this was a part of a campaign of "cultural cleansing". According to EEPA, the monks' ancient dwellings and the earliest existing church in Ethiopia still in its original style were also "completely destroyed".[159]

April 2021 A priest, who remained anonymous for security reasons, revealed that hundreds lay dead in Tigray, with priests having been beaten up and churches ransacked. The source said there had been a lot of violence against priests and Sisters. He added that in his own area "three parish priests have been threatened and beaten" and all the property of the parishes has been "completely cleaned out by the soldiers."[160]

May 2021 The head of the Ethiopian Orthodox Tewahedo Church has said the Ethiopian government "want to destroy the people of Tigray" with actions of "the highest brutality and cruelty", adding it was unclear why Ethiopia wanted to "declare genocide on the people of Tigray".[161]

May 2021 An unnamed source told ACN that nuns were among women who had been raped as part of the attack on the Tigray region. The source said: "Our sisters have been raped. Some of them we had to take to hospital, even nuns have been raped."[162]

July 2021 Tigrayan clerics said that over 300 religious leaders – including priests, monks and Muslims – had been killed by the government's military operation in the region.[163] The EEPA released testimony from a priest from Tigray who said that "up to the 4th May 2021, the total number of religious leaders killed during their religious service are more than 326".[164] He also said that, "we heard that two girls, who were in the formation to become Sisters, were raped by 18 soldiers."

October 2021 A Catholic nun reported being raped by three Eritrean soldiers. Sister Tiemtu Afewerki, a Tigrayan nun, used to live in Jerusalem but returned to Tigray to look after her dead sister's children. "Three PFDJ [government] soldiers raped me," she said, before adding that they shot her nieces dead and threw them into the Tekeze river.[165]

November 2021 Priests and their wives are being targeted by soldiers – according to Helen Berhane. The Christian, who was formerly imprisoned for her faith in Eritrea, warned that hostility towards Christians is overflowing from Eritrea into Tigray. She said: "Eritrean troops are killing a lot of priests and raping their wives." She added: "Some of the priests stand holding their crosses, so they cut their hands. And when the soldiers ask the priests to remove their hats, when they say no, they shoot them. Hundreds of priests are dying in this conflict at the hands of Eritrean soldiers".[166]

July 2022 Bishops in Ethiopia warned that churches have been shut down, with priests and nuns forced to flee, because of the insecurity in Tigray.[167] Cardinal Berhaneyesus Demerew Souraphiel, chairman of the Ethiopian bishops' conference, said "Priests and Sisters have fled their monasteries due to (in)security, and the number of closed chapels and monasteries is increasing".[168]

INDIA

Population
1.38 billion

Religions
Hindus	72.5%
Muslims	14.5%
Christians	5%
Tribal religions	3.5%
Sikhs	1.75%
Other	2.75%

Christian Population
68 million

© Ismael Martínez Sánchez / ACN

Attacks on Christians reached a record high during the period under review. The United Christian Forum of Human Rights recorded 505 incidences of violence and hate in 2021 – up from 279 in 2020 – and 302 in the first seven months of 2022. A common theme was the failure of police to intervene or prosecute perpetrators.[169] In 2021, the largest number of cases were reported in the north, with 102 in Uttar Pradesh, 90 in Chhattisgarh, 44 in Jharkhand and 38 in Madhya Pradesh. However, the scale of these attacks may be higher, and another report recorded at least 761 incidents of violence against Christians during 2021.[170]

Many attacks are driven by allegations of conversion, and anti-conversion laws play a role in these. Ten states have passed or updated laws prohibiting religious conversion by deception or force. Uttar Pradesh and Madhya Pradesh both recently introduced anti-conversion laws. In Madhya Pradesh this played some part in the 75 arrests of Christians in the month following the anti-conversion legislation – the Freedom of Religion Act – coming into effect in January 2021.[171] Dilip Chouhan, who is part of a radical Hindutva group that has attacked church services in Madhya Pradesh, told the *New York Times:* "These 'believers' they promise all kinds of stuff — motorcycles, TVs, fridges. They work off superstition. They mislead people." Emboldened by new anti-conversion laws, his group broke up a Church service in Alirajpur in February 2021. Police officers accompanied them. Footage shows Mr Chouhan entering the church with a shotgun on his back.[172] In May 2022 at least 30 Christians were jailed in Uttar Pradesh State – including 20 in the last week of the month – on charges of forced conversion.[173] The United Christian Forum's A. C. Michael said: "The enactment of laws in the name of freedom of religion exacerbates the situation. It would not be an exaggeration to say that these events are well-orchestrated and planned acts by some groups with the aim of dividing the country based on religious issues."[174]

Much of the anti-Christian rhetoric fuelling attacks dwells on the idea that Hindus are on the way to being outnumbered in India, a neurotic fear prompted by 2015 census data showing that for the first time since the founding of modern India in 1947, Hindus had dropped below 80 percent of the population. In October 2021 Mohan Bhagwat, head of the Hindutva group Rashtriya Swayamsevak Sangh (RSS) warned Hindus about the "unnatural growth" of the country's Christian and Muslim populations,[175] before telling hearers at his annual speech during the days of Navaratri (a festival honouring the Hindu deity Durga): "Illegal immigration in bordering districts and conversions in [the] northeast have changed the demographics further."[176] The spread of Hindutva philosophy espoused by RSS is, to a large extent, the cause of growing persecution against Christians. Hindutva is a right-wing form of Hindu nationalism, which essentially regards India as a Hindu country which should not tolerate other religions or cultures. The Bharatiya Janata Party (BJP), which took power in 2014, subscribes to this ideological approach and its political success has facilitated right-wing rhetoric and action.

October 2020 A cross was pulled down and a Hindu shrine put up in its place in Madanpur village in Chhattisgarh State's Korba district. Christians had gathered to pray there for more than two decades.

November 2020 Uttar Pradesh passed a law stipulating that those intending to convert must give 60-days notice to the district magistrate. The burden of proving a conversion was genuine falls upon the individual converting or the religious authorities who received them. Government spokesperson Sidharth Nath Singh claimed to be aware of around 100 incidents of "forced conversion", but provided no specifics.[177]

January 2021 On the morning of Wednesday 26th, a group of men shouting Hindutva slogans entered the Satprakashan Sanchar Kendra Christian Centre, Indore, Madhya Pradesh. Pastor Manish David said: "They kept beating us, pulling out hair." Police arrived and arrested nine elders, including Pastor David, charging them under new legislation restricting religious conversions. Pastor David said that, during the two months he was in jail, officials denied him access to a lawyer. On several occasions he was also denied food and water.[178]

September 2021 Police in Uttar Pradesh beat two Christians in custody with lathi, heavy iron-bound bamboo sticks. Sabajeet and Chotelal from Sultanpur District were accused under the state's 2020 anti-conversion laws. They were told by the station chief that they had betrayed India by converting to Christianity. They were released later that night without charge.[179]

October 2021 Christ Jyoti Senior Secondary School in Madhya Pradesh's Satna District was ordered to place a statue of the Hindu goddess Saraswati within its grounds. Around 30 men from Vishwa Hindu Parishad (VHP) and Bajrang Dal told school manager Father Augustine Chittuparambil that there had been an image of the goddess on the property, until it was removed three years ago. School authorities insisted there had never been a statue of Saraswati on the site, which opened in 1973.[180]

October 2021 Listeners were urged to kill Christians by Hindu religious leader Swami Parmatmanand during a mass rally in Chhattisgarh's Surguja district. He said: "Behead them – those who come for conversion." As he counselled violence, local BJP political leaders including Ramvichar Netam and Nand Kumar Sai were with him on stage. The latter was videoed applauding the swami. The Bandh Karo Dharmantaran (Stop Religious Conversions) rally was organised by Sarwa Sanatan Hindu Raksha Manch, a loose coalition of Hindutva groups.[181]

Christians in Madhya Pradesh

December 2021 Christian books were burned by extremists in Kolar, Karnataka State, after being taken from Christians distributing them to households as part of an evangelistic outreach. One of those involved in the book burning said they "did not act violently", adding: "We did not trouble them. They were distributing books in our neighbourhood and were propagating about Christianity". This was the 38th attack on religious minorities in Karnataka in 2021. Attacks increased following discussions by the BJP-dominated state government about introducing a bill to ban forced conversions. A police officer said: "We have warned the Christian community to not create any communal disharmony by going door-to-door and preaching. Both parties, the right wing and the Christian community members have settled the matter amicably". No arrests were made.[182]

December 2021 St Joseph's School in Ganj Basoda, Madhya Pradesh State was ransacked by a mob of around 500 Hindutva extremists on 6th December – after school authorities requested police protection. School principal Brother Anthony Pynumkal said that around midday a mob armed with iron rods and stones arrived. They chanted Hindu slogans while vandalising school property. The incident was preceded by accusations posted by "Aayudh" on YouTube that the school was converting Hindu students. The post showed photos of eight Catholic children receiving Confirmation and First Holy Communion at the parish church, but it was alleged to show the conversion of Hindu pupils at the school. The Syro-Malabar Catholic Church's Malabar Missionary Brothers (MMB) run the school, which today has 1,500 students, of whom less than one percent are Christians. Father Maria Stephen told ACN: "The police indirectly supported the mob. The school administration submitted an application for protection a day before but they did not take it seriously. There was a feeling that the superintendent of police did not like the Christians." The vandals destroyed school property for more than an hour before police finally intervened. Brother Pynumkal also alleged that there were inaccuracies in the first information report (FIR) filed by officers, estimating the mob to be only 100, and reporting the damage was around

₹800,000 rather than more than ₹2 million. BJP-run Madhya Pradesh is one of ten states in India with a law prohibiting religious conversion.[183]

December 2021 Models of Santa Claus were burnt after being stolen from outside Christian schools in Agra, Uttar Pradesh by members of Antarrashtriya Hindu Parishad and Rashtriya Bajrang Dal. Ajju Chauhan, regional general secretary of Bajrang Dal, said: "As December comes, the Christian missionaries become active in the name of Christmas, Santa Claus and New Year. They lure children by making Santa Claus distribute gifts to them and attract them towards Christianity".[184]

January 2022 On Sunday 9th, a house church was attacked by a 200-strong mob in Kondagaon District, Chhattisgarh. Hindutva extremist Sanjith Ng broke into the house in Odagaon village where a service was taking place and attacked members of the congregation. He dragged Pastor Hemanth Kandapan outside, where the minister and Christian man Sankar Salam were beaten. Both needed hospital treatment for their injuries. The pastor alleged police were present, but did not intervene. Members of the mob claimed the church was illegally converting Hindus, and said they would kill Christians if they continued to meet in the village. The following day, senior members of Vishwa Hindu Parishad (VHP) made Christian villagers attend a Ghar Wapsi event. It was reported that one woman, Sunderi Bathi, was forcibly converted to Hinduism.[185]

February 2022 Police officer, Sub-Inspector Bhavesh Shende, oversaw the torching of a church building in Kistaram village, Chhattisgarh State. Shende disrupted worship on Thursday 3rd, telling Christians to stop praying and threatening to charge them as Maoist rebels. The following evening, senior church members Gurva and Turram Kanna were summoned to Kistaram police station where they refused demands to burn down their church. It was torched the following day.[186]

March 2022 A candle-lit protest along the roads between Catholic Churches in Mangaluru and Dakshina Kannada on Wednesday 2nd highlighted attacks on Christians following the introduction of anti-conversion legislation by Karnataka's state government in December 2021. Among the attacks in February were the illegal demolition of the hall attached to St Antony's Church, which had been on that site for more than 40 years, and the destruction by authorities of a 20-foot (six-metre) high statue of Jesus set up in Gokunte village in 2004.[187]

March 2022 Christian pastor Yalam Sankar was stabbed to death on Thursday 17th after being dragged out of his house in Angampalli village, Chhattisgarh State by five men. The 50-year-old minister had received death threats from Hindutva extremists, who ordered him to stop preaching Christianity. Father Vincent Ekka disputed police claims he was killed by Naxals, local Maoist militants.[188]

April 2022 In Karnataka State, Vishwa Hindu Parishad (VHP) and Bajrang Dal called for Christian chaplains to be banned from prisons.[189]

April 2022 On the evening of Maundy Thursday 55 Christians were detained for "illegal conversions". A 200-strong mob stopped more than 70 members of the Evangelical Church of India from leaving the grounds of their nineteenth-century church in Fatehpur, Uttar Pradesh. When police arrived, they questioned the Christians for three hours before charging and taking 55 to the station. 26 men were kept overnight in cells and taken to court the following day: 17 of these were remanded in custody before being released on Holy Saturday. Police reportedly withdrew all conversion charges – but charged them with violations of the Penal Code. Church sources said Hindutva leaders: "portrayed [the service] as a religious conversion activity and those who attended it were harassed for no fault of their own."[190]

May 2022 A mob dragged a Protestant pastor out of the prayer hall where he was leading worship in the Jaunpur district of Uttar Pradesh on Tuesday 31st. Police arrested the pastor under section 295a of the Indian Penal Code (deliberate and malicious acts, aimed at outraging religious feelings). He was released on bail on 3rd June.[191]

August 2022 More than 150 Sikhs disrupted an Evangelical Christian event in Daduana village in Punjab's Amritsar district on Monday 29th, beating the organisers. The next day Sikh leader Harpreet Singh, the acting Jathedar of Akal Takht, publicly supported the assailants and called for charges against them to be dropped. He repeated Hindutva narratives about Christians conducting forced conversions. Following the Jathedar's statement, four masked youths attacked a Catholic Church in Tarn Taran District.

IRAN

The constitution of Iran defines the country as an Islamic republic, with the official state religion being Twelver Ja'afari Shia Islam.[192] The penal code punishes proselytising by non-Muslims with the death sentence; "enmity against God" and "insulting the Prophet or Islam" are also punishable by death.[193]

According to the constitution, Christians are one of the few religious minorities that are permitted to worship and form religious societies "within the limits of the law", but this does not include converts from Islam.[194] The only permitted conversions are from other religions to Islam.[195] The government considers any citizen who cannot prove that they or their family were Christian prior to 1979 to be Muslim.[196] The law prevents Muslim citizens from changing or renouncing their religious beliefs.[197] Christian converts are not allowed to legally register themselves as Christians and are not entitled to the same rights as recognised members of Christian communities.[198] There are believed to be just 800,000 Christians in Iran, making them a tiny minority. Converts to Christianity are viewed with deep suspicion as they are seen as an attempt by Western countries to undermine Islam and the Islamic regime of Iran.

The treatment of Christian convert Fatemeh (Mary) Mohammadi in January 2020 is fairly typical: during protests in central Tehran, she was

POPULATION	**CHRISTIAN POPULATION**	
83.6 million	800,000	

RELIGIONS
Muslims 98.5%   Christians 0.75%   Baha'is 0.25%   Others 0.5%

taken to Vozara Detention Centre, and beaten so severely by male and female prison guards that she carried visible bruises for three weeks.[199] On January 18th 2021, she was rearrested by the morality police, who said her trousers were too tight, her headscarf was not correctly adjusted, and her coat shouldn't be unbuttoned.[200]

In September 2020, a Christian Iranian couple who adopted a daughter had the child taken from them and were declared "unfit" to be parents because they are not Muslim.[201] The couple, Sam Khosravi and Maryam Falahi, are facing other legal challenges, with Mr Khosravi sentenced to a year in prison and two years in internal exile for "propaganda against the state", for the couple's attendance at an illegal house church.[202]

The legal situation for Christians worsened in February 2021 when President Hassan Rouhani signed amendments to articles 499 and 500 of the penal code, introducing prison sentences for those guilty of "insulting Islam" and undertaking "deviant activity" that "contradicts or interferes with the sacred law of Islam".[203] This adds to the fact that underground Christians are often imprisoned on charges of "sectarian activities" or "engaging in propaganda against the Islamic regime".[204] ,

The NGO Article 18 reported that, on 19th April 2021, intelligence agents in Dezful, Khuzestan Province, arrested four Church of Iran converts – Hojjat Lotfi Khalaf, Esmaeil Narimanpour, Alireza Varak-Shah, and Mohammad Ali (Davoud) Torabi.[205] In August they were charged with "propaganda against the Islamic Republic" on the grounds of their membership of a house church.

In its 2022 Annual Report, the United States Commission on International Religious Freedom (USCIRF) recommended that Iran be re-designated as a "country of particular concern" for its treatment of religious minorities, including Christians.[206]

February 2021 11 Christian families were summoned by authorities, interrogated and then warned to stop their house church meetings. They were also warned not to visit each other at home, even for social gatherings.[207]

April 2021 Four Church of Iran converts were arrested and interrogated by intelligence agents in the southwestern city of Dezful.[208] Hojjat Lotfi Khalaf, Esmaeil Narimanpour, Alireza Varak-Shah, and Mohammad Ali (Davoud) Torabi, were arrested on 19th April.

June 2021 Three members of the Church of Iran were charged with "sectarian activities" under a recent amendment to the Iranian penal code.[209] Esmaeil and Hojjat were arrested during morning raids on their homes, while Davoud was detained after intelligence agents came to his shop, then took him with them to search his home.

September 2021 Amin Khaki, Milad Goudarzi and Alireza Nourmohammadi had prison sentences reduced to three years by the 12th Chamber of the Court of Appeal of the Revolutionary Tribunal in Karaj. The three members of the Church of Iran were first sentenced to five years in prison in June for "engaging in propaganda against the Islamic regime" and also stood trial for engaging in "sectarian activities".[210]

January 2022 Pastor Matthias (Abdulreza Ali) Hagnejad was re-arrested two weeks after being released from prison pending a review of his five-year sentence.[211] He was released in late December 2021 after nearly three years in prison on charges of "endangering state security" and "promoting Zionist Christianity".[212] Eight other Church of Iran members were arrested at the same time.[213]

February 2022 Intelligence agents in Iran's Khuzestan Province instructed 10 Christian converts who had been cleared of all charges to participate in "re-education" classes led by Islamic clerics, according to Article 18, a non-profit NGO that promotes religious freedom and tolerance for Christians in Iran.[214]

February 2022 Two Christian converts in Tehran had their request for a retrial rejected after they were given custodial sentences for practising their faith.[215] Hadi Rahimi and Sakineh Behjati were summoned to begin their four-and two-year sentences on 16th February after Branch 9 of the Supreme Court rejected their appeal. The pair were sentenced to prison by Branch 26 of the Tehran Revolutionary Court in August 2020 on the official charge of "membership of groups seeking to disrupt the national security." It is highly likely that the pair were targeted because they attended a house church.

March 2022 Nine Christian converts were acquitted by an appeals court after previously being charged with "acting against national security" and "promoting Zionist Christianity".[216] Judges Seyed Ali Asghar Kamali and Akbar Johari said there was "insufficient evidence" to show that the accused had acted against state security, and argued that Christians are taught to live in "obedience, submission and support of the authorities".

April 2022 Pastor Yousef Nadarkhani was granted five days of temporary furlough from prison so he could spend time with his family. Pastor Nadarkhani was arrested with three other members of the Church of Iran during raids by security agents on Christian homes in May 2016. He is serving a six-year sentence on charges of "acting against national security" by "promoting Zionist Christianity".[217]

May 2022 Three Christians were sentenced to prison, or exile, after being accused of forming a "house church". A Tehran Revolutionary Court sentenced Iranian-Armenian Anooshavan Avedian to 10 years in prison and 10 years of "deprivation of social rights" for teaching Christians in his home. Christian converts Abbas Soori, 45, and Maryam Mohammadi, 46, were also deprived of social rights for 10 years and fined 500 million rials (£9,800). They were also banned from leaving Iran.[218]

IRAQ

A fact-finding and project-assessment trip to Iraq by Aid to the Church in Need (ACN) in March 2022 found significant progress had been made to stabilise the Christian community after genocidal violence at the hands of Daesh (ISIS). But, despite improvements, the situation "remained concerning",[219] with considerable threats posing serious questions about the Church's long-term survival.

Daesh remained an underlying concern, with research suggesting "Iraq sees the most [Daesh] activity, which is not surprising given the group's Iraqi origins and the Iraqi complexion of its leadership." Attacks include "small-arms assaults, ambushes, roadside bombings, suicide bombings, assassinations, kidnappings and acts of sabotage".[220] Amid reports from military experts that Daesh "continues to be a highly active and lethal insurgent force in the Middle East particularly in rural Iraq and Syria",[221] there remains the threat of a large-scale violent outbreak, potentially involving territorial gain. Such an incident could have existential consequences for Iraq's Christians, who in a generation have been decimated from 1.2 million to perhaps 150,000 today.[222] Even in Baghdad the relatively strong Christian presence of the 1960s onwards has "dropped substantively over the last years [and] many churches have reportedly closed down".[223]

Despite these and other challenges – including "rampant unemployment"[224] – the return of up to 60 percent of internally displaced Christians and other minorities to their homelands in the Nineveh Plains has been enabled

by a massive rebuilding campaign. But many others have abandoned plans to return amid signs of militia presence in the region, hostile to Christians. Militia, some backed by Iran and acting under the auspices of the state-backed Popular Mobilisation Units, harassed Christians wanting to return.[225] Shabak Shi'a militia expropriated large tracts of agricultural land owned by Christians, including in and around Bartella on the Nineveh Plains.[226]

Several years on from Daesh's defeat, barely 50 Christian families had gone back to Mosul as of March 2022.[227] During a visit to Mosul in May 2020, Prime Minister Mustafa Al-Kadhimi said "Christians represent one of the most authentic components of Iraq and it saddens us to see them leave the country".[228] In spite of such statements of support, many Christians in Mosul expressed mistrust of former Muslim neighbours and concerns about Daesh sleeper cells,[229] making the prospect of a wholesale return of Christians to Mosul very unlikely.

But, while the position for Christians in some parts of Nineveh remains uncertain, the situation for formerly displaced Christian communities now settled in Ankawa was strengthened when the Erbil suburb was granted administrative control *(see June 2021)*. The creation of a new Syriac Catholic Archdiocese in Ankawa is further evidence that the area has transformed from being a place of displacement to becoming a permanent home.[230] In the extreme north, Christian villages suffered Turkish raids apparently aimed at Kurdish forces near Iraq's northerly border. Villages such as Chalik, Bersiveh and Sharanish were reportedly among the worst affected. Local Christian organisations claimed these attacks sought to empty the area of people as part of Turkey's plans to create bases to launch ground operations against the PKK (Kurdish Workers' Party).[231]

Iraq's 2005 constitution contains ambiguities, both protecting the religious rights of Christians and other minorities (Article 2 (2)) and stating "Islam is the official state religion and a source of legislation." (Article 2 (1)).[232] Church leaders said that minorities do not feel equal before the law. Chaldean Catholic Patriarch Louis Raphael I Sako of Baghdad called on the

government "to enact a law that respects freedom of conscience" and follow "the example of [countries] which have repealed the law of apostasy".[233] But, the government did take some steps to recognise religions other than Islam: for example, making Christmas a national holiday *(see December 2020).*[234]

Despite the challenges facing Iraq's Christians, Pope Francis's March 2021 visit gave hope to the faithful. Of particular significance was his meeting with Grand Ayatollah Ali Al-Sistani, the country's most senior Shi'a cleric. The significant security laid on for the visit emphasised the threats that still exist.[235]

December 2020 The Iraqi Parliament voted unanimously to establish Christmas as an annual national holiday. Previously, 25th December was recognised as a Christian holiday but not a national public holiday.[236]

March 2021 Pope Francis became the first Pope to visit Iraq. During the four-day trip, he went to Ur. Abraham came from Ur in the Bible. The trip also involved visits to churches and other structures damaged by Daesh.[237]

March 2021 Iraq Prime Minister Mustafa Al-Kadhimi declared 6th March as the annual National Day of Tolerance and Coexistence in Iraq. Announcing the yearly celebration, the Prime Minister stated that it was intended "in celebration of the historic meeting in Najaf between Ayatollah Ali Al-Sistani and Pope Francis, and the historic inter-religious meeting in the ancient city of Ur."[238]

May 2021 Turkish forces were accused of destroying a church and several buildings in a bombing raid on Miska, a Christian village in the

Amedi district of Dohuk province. It was reported that three villages had now been abandoned as a result of the incessant bombing.[239]

June 2021 Ankawa, the largely Christian suburb of Erbil, was designated an official district by Masrour Barzani, Prime Minister of Iraq's Kurdistan region. The decision means that residents of the district have "administrative control" instead of being under the direct authority of the Mayor of Erbil. Powers delegated to Ankawa include the right to elect officials and representatives, the right to manage its own administration and the right to provide for its own security and provide welfare support.[240]

July 2021 USCIRF praised the US State Department's announcement of an additional US$155 million in humanitarian assistance for Iraq, contributing to US$200 million for the fiscal year 2021. The aid will support Iraqis displaced by Daesh, including religious minorities.[241]

November 2021 The home of a Christian shopkeeper in Al-Amarah, south-east Iraq, was attacked with improvised bombs. The shopkeeper had an official licence to sell alcohol in his shop but nonetheless had been the victim of numerous threats. Al-Amarah is home to only eight Christian families: the others have fled.[242]

June 2022 Iran was accused in a report of carrying out an "invisible jihad" against Christians in Iraq and other countries, aimed at driving them out of the Middle East. According to a report by the Philos Project, "Iran's proxy militias in Lebanon, Iraq, Syria and Yemen have played a significant, though largely unrecognised, role in the dramatic decline of Christians in the region." The report claims that militias "laboured to create conditions that forced the Christians out".[243]

August 2022 Patriarch Louis Raphael I Sako, head of the Chaldean Catholic Church, warned that Christians could disappear from the country unless governmental, social and economic policies change. Speaking on the first day of a Church Synod in Baghdad, he said: "Iraqi Christians, and perhaps also Christians of other nations, will soon disappear if there is no change in thinking and of the state system." He said Islamic heritage in Iraq "makes Christians second-class citizens and allows the usurpation of their property", and repeated calls for the constitution to be changed.[244]

Iraq

Building a Future

CATHOLIC UNIVERSITY ERBIL

The Catholic University in Erbil (CUE) is critical to the recovery of Iraq in the wake of the genocidal violence that the people suffered at the hands of the Islamist militants from Daesh (ISIS).

Established by Archbishop Bashar Warda of Erbil, CUE welcomes students from all cultures, religions and educational backgrounds in an environment committed to academic excellence, mutual respect and friendship.

Aid to the Church in Need has been a major project partner in the development of CUE. As well as providing funding for Laboratory Medical Science, one of a growing number of academic departments, ACN has supported 150 students on the Pope Francis Scholarship Programme.[245]

When ACN staff visited CUE on a project-assessment trip, they met first-year student Joudy, a Christian from Aleppo. 18-year-old Joudy, *(pictured left)* who narrowly escaped being killed when a bomb landed near her school, left Syria with her family and sought sanctuary in Iraq's Christian-majority district of Ankawa, part of the Kurdish semi-autonomous capital of Erbil.

She told ACN: "My dream is to be an architect. I imagine one day being able to play my part in building up my city once again. I remember how beautiful it used to be."[246]

ISRAEL AND THE PALESTINIAN TERRITORIES

© Ismael Martínez Sánchez / ACN

Population
Combined figures
for both polities
14 million

Religions
Jews	49%
Muslims	43.5%
Agnostics	5%
Christians	1.5%
Other	1%

Christian Population
217,000

In December 2021 the patriarchs and heads of local Churches in Jerusalem wrote that:

> Throughout the Holy Land, Christians have become the target of frequent and sustained attacks by fringe radical groups. Since 2012 there have been countless incidents of physical and verbal assaults against priests and other clergy, attacks on Christian churches, with holy sites regularly vandalised and desecrated, and ongoing intimidation of local Christians who simply seek to worship freely and go about their daily lives. These tactics are being used by such radical groups in a systematic attempt to drive the Christian community out of Jerusalem and other parts of the Holy Land. [247]

They added that the unique spiritual and cultural character of Jerusalem's historic quarters needed to be protected, pointing out that "radical groups continue to acquire strategic property in the Christian Quarter, with the aim of diminishing the Christian presence, often using underhanded dealings and intimidation tactics". Writing in the *Daily Telegraph*, Fr Francesco Patton, Custos of the Holy Land wrote: "These radical groups do not represent the government or the people of Israel. But as with any extremist faction, a radical minority can too easily burden the lives of many, especially if their activities go unchecked and their crimes are unpunished." He wrote that churches had been desecrated and priests, monks and worshippers targeted. Stuart Winer writing in the *Times of Israel* commented:

> Though neither Patton nor the Church leaders statement mentioned it by name, Ateret Cohanim is a religious-Zionist organisation that works to populate the Old City and other East Jerusalem neighbourhoods with Jewish residents by purchasing properties from non-Jewish owners. Separately, extremist Jewish activists have for years carried out vandalism against Christian sites in Jerusalem and other areas of Israel, including hate graffiti and arson. The extremists also target Palestinians.[248]

There is a history of extremist attacks, and in 2015, Benzi Gopstein, leader of the Jewish far-right group Lehava, publicly called for churches to be torched.[249]

There were 182,000 Christians in Israel in 2021, according to its Central Bureau of Statistics. Most belong to the Melkite Greek Catholic Church (*c.* 60 percent). While the overall Christian population of Israel is growing – increasing by 1.4 percent last year – in the Palestinian Territories historic Christian communities continue to decline. Before the State of Israel was established in 1948, Christians made up 18 percent of the population of the West Bank: that figure is now less than 1 percent. Reasons for emigration are various, including concerns about discrimination in employment, militant groups like Hamas, and restrictions on movement caused by the West Bank Barrier which gives rise to major economic problems.

December 2020 a 49-year-old Jewish man was arrested for an arson attack on the Church of All Nations, Gethsemane.[250]

February-March 2021 The Romanian Orthodox Monastery in Jerusalem suffered four attacks in the space of a month, culminating in an arson attempt which gutted the church entrance. The Assembly of Catholic Ordinaries of the Holy Land accused extremist Jewish settlers. [251]

August 2021 A six-inch (15.25 cm) tall iron cross, embedded in an outdoor altar, was stolen from the Church of the Multiplication of Loaves and Fishes, Tabgha. The basalt rock altar was on the shore of the Sea of Galilee, in part of the church's grounds closed to the public at the time. Georg Röwekamp of the German Association of the Holy Land, which owns the property, said: "As this requires strong physical force, it must have been a deliberate act". In 2015, more than £850,000 of damage was caused to the church by an arson attack.[252]

October 2021 Israeli authorities shut down three days of children's events at the Catholic institution Abraham's House in East Jerusalem. The programme was sponsored by the United Nations Development Programme, Finland's Ministry for Foreign Affairs and the Austrian Development Corporation. Children were watching a puppet show when plain-clothes police arrived on Tuesday 26th and stopped proceedings on the grounds the organisers had received backing from the Palestinian National Authority (PA). PA-sponsored events are prohibited in East Jerusalem, but organisers insisted no support was received from them. The decision to stop the events was made by the Israeli Minister of Internal Security. A seminar for Christians and Jews on Vatican II's inter-faith document Nostra Aetate scheduled for the end of October was cancelled following the incident.[253]

February 2022 Plans to incorporate Church sites on the Mount of Olives into a new national park were suspended by the Israel Nature and Parks Authority. In a letter to Environmental Protection Minister Tamar Zandberg, Church leaders said proposals would "confiscate and nationalise one of the holiest sites for Christianity and alter its nature." The authority said future proposals would not be discussed by the planning committee without consultation with Christian leaders.[254]

March 2022 Ateret Cohanim occupied part of Little Petra Hotel, over which they have been in a long-running legal battle with the Greek Orthodox Patriarchate. They broke into the pilgrim hostel near the Jaffa Gate on Saturday 26th, taking possession of the first floor the following day. Police allegedly supported Ateret Cohanim, preventing hostel guests and lawyers from entering, and arrested three Palestinians.[255]

April 2022 After spending 40 days in prison for meeting with a former member of the Israeli parliament, Christian Pastor Johnny Shahwan was released by the Palestinian National Authority on Monday 11th. Pastor Shahwan, who ran Beit Al-Liqa, which provides faith-based programmes for local families, was arrested after a visit by former Knesset member Rabbi Yehudah Glick. According to The Jerusalem Post, Shahwan was charged with "undermining the national sentiments [of Palestinians], stirring up sectarian strife and insulting the prestige of the [Palestinian] state." If convicted he would have faced hard labour.[256]

April 2022 Worshippers attending Greek Orthodox Easter Vigil services in the Church of the Holy Sepulchre were restricted to 4,000 – the patriarchate claimed up to 11,000 usually attended. Israeli authorities said the move was prompted by health and safety concerns, after 45 died during a stampede on Mount Meron during the Jewish Lag Ba'Omer festival attended by *c.* 100,000 people in 2021. The patriarchate said it was "fed up with police restrictions on freedom to worship."[257]

May 2022 Bishops condemned Israeli Police for using heavy-handed tactics against mourners in the funeral procession of Melkite Greek Catholic journalist Shireen Abu Akleh. Security camera footage released by St Joseph's Hospital, where the funeral procession began, showed dozens of officers in riot gear entering the hospital. More than 100 officers gathered outside, using smoke grenades and rubber bullets on mourners, as well as hitting them with batons. Israeli Police insisted officers were dealing with individuals "disrupting public order" following stone throwing and later tweeted support for officers.[258]

June 2022 Around 50 Jewish extremists broke into the Greek Orthodox Patriarchate of Jerusalem's chapel on the hill of Zion around 10.30am on Monday 6th. The Patriarchate had locked the complex, having had extremists camp in the gardens ahead of the Jewish feast of Shavuot (Weeks) in previous years. The patriarchate said the chapel had been "defiled" but gave no specifics – previously radicals had urinated in the chapel and graffitied it. The extremists threatened to kill a guard who tried to stop them.[259]

July 2022 140 priests on pilgrimage were reportedly attacked by ultra-Orthodox Jews when they stopped in Jerusalem's Jewish Quarter. Police were accused of not intervening.

September 2022 Religious extremism, military occupation, discrimination and "systematic violations of human rights" are among the factors threatening vulnerable communities, including Christians according to a statement from the the eleventh Assembly of the World Council of Churches. Israeli authorities were criticised for failing to protect the Christian presence in Jerusalem.[260]

Israel/Palestine

Building Bridges

Young people learning to build bridges on the Rossing Centre's "Healing Hatred" programme

The Holy Land is beset by religious, socio-political and economic tensions which have led to violence. Promoting dialogue and building bridges between the different groups is a vital task – and one that Aid to the Church in Need is supporting through the work of the Rossing Centre in Jerusalem, having backed it with more than £400,000 in project support.

Among the initiatives ACN has supported is the programme "Develop Forgiveness, Overcome Hatred" which draws together hundreds of young Christians, Jews and Muslims and helps them to learn to live and look to the future together.

The Latin Patriarch of Jerusalem, Metropolitan Pierbattista Pizzaballa praised the charity for its work: "I would like to thank ACN, because the pastoral charity does a great deal in the Holy Land. It supports many projects, including "Develop Forgiveness, Overcome Hatred", which is organised by the Rossing Center. Daniel Rossing was a Jew who felt that Jerusalem in particular needed to be a place where all religions felt at home.

"Many young people who participate in these classes apply what they learn in their professional lives. Which makes religion, which is often an element of division in the Holy Land, an element of unity."

MALDIVES

Image: Jonathan Palombo

Maldives has an international reputation as a perfect holiday destination, but life is far from idyllic for the country's Christians. Away from the tourist attractions, Christians suffer severe persecution for their faith.[261] Every aspect of their lives is so heavily restricted that they are largely forced underground. Indeed, being a Christian in the Maldives is so "dangerous", it is reported that individuals conceal their faith from their family members.[262]

Article 9d of the constitution states that "a non-Muslim may not become a citizen of the Maldives"[263] and hence "the official statistics"[264] show the country is 100 percent Muslim. However, there could be up to 95,000 immigrants – 25 percent of the population[265], of whom Christians could "number a few hundred".[266]

That there should be no precise data about the Christian population reflects the level of repression experienced by a community who, as non-citizens, have no rights. The Protection of Religious Unity Act 1994 makes it illegal to "display in public symbols or slogans belonging to a religion other than Islam" (Article 6)[267]. Similarly, there is a ban on promoting faiths other than Islam in books and other texts (Article 7).[268] For this reason, importing Bibles and other Christian literature is forbidden[269]

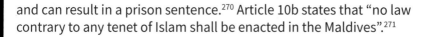

POPULATION
459,000

CHRISTIAN POPULATION
Unknown

RELIGIONS
Muslims 99%   Others 1%

and can result in a prison sentence.[270] Article 10b states that "no law contrary to any tenet of Islam shall be enacted in the Maldives".[271]

The punishment for breaking these laws is between two and five years in jail for Maldivians. *Shari'a* law-inspired punishments mandated by the Penal Code include "flogging, stoning, and amputation of hands."[272] It is against the law for a Muslim to convert. Sentences include possible loss of citizenship but "a judge may impose a harsher punishment [as] per Shari'a jurisprudence" which may be interpreted by religious scholars as approving the use of the death penalty in extreme cases.[273]

Non-Muslims, including Christians, visiting from abroad also face severe penalties. If they are found to have broken these laws, for example by displaying non-Islamic religious symbols or importing Bibles, foreigners "must be handed over to the Ministry of Immigration and Emigration for expulsion from the Maldives."[274]

During the reporting period, there was no sign of any decrease in surveillance and reporting of activities suspected of being pro-Christian or supportive of a non-Muslim faith. The Ministry of Islamic Affairs "continued to maintain control over all matters associated with religious activity and belief". There was a ban on the import of items seen as a threat to Islam. Literature, religious statues, alcohol and pork products are not allowed, and violations can carry sentences of up to three years. A male citizen may marry a non-Muslim foreigner, provided the individual is Christian or Jewish. If not, the person must convert to Islam before being married.[275]

Problems for Christians in the Maldives do not come just from the state. There were continuing signs that pro-jihadist Islam had a strong foothold in society. Reports indicated that the country had "one of the highest per capita numbers of militants who fought in Syria and Iraq".[276] In August 2020, the Maldives Journalists' Association published a

survey in which 37 percent of the 70 journalists who took part described "being labelled 'irreligious' and threatened by radicalised and sometimes extremist individuals or groups online".[277] Evidence of extremist-inspired violence included the May 2021 attack on Parliament Speaker Mohamed Nasheed.[278] In June 2022, police used pepper spray to disperse crowds who disrupted an event marking international yoga day, brandishing placards condemning the initiative as anti-Islamic.[279] The presence of militant, extremist Muslims in society means that for Christians and other minorities there is no guarantee of peace and acceptance even away from the prying eyes of state oppression. The influence of hard-line Islamic organisations, including the Adhaalath Party, represents a threat to Christians and other religious minorities. In 2019, Adhaalath succeeded in pressurising the government to close the Maldivian Democracy Network, a human rights NGO. An official press release from the Maldivian Ministry of Foreign Affairs described the network's reports as containing "content slandering Islam and the Prophet Mohamed (PBUH)."[280]

November 2020 The Criminal Court ordered all local internet service providers to block access to websites, social media pages, YouTube channels, and online applications that targeted Maldivians "with the intention of spreading religions other than Islam." The order was issued by the authorities following reports that Christian advertising in the local Dhivehi language aimed at children had appeared on Facebook, YouTube and certain gaming apps.[281]

December 2020 The Ministry of Islamic Affairs (MIA) filed a police case against Clique College in the capital Malé for "playing Christian songs at a children's sports festival" which took place in the Hulhumale Central Park. The lyrics included: "We believe in Jesus. We believe in the Holy Spirit." In a statement, the MIA described the incident as "a very serious matter". The college stated the song "accidentally auto-played from a playlist and the organisers immediately changed the song upon realising that it was Christian."[282]

May 2021 Police described the attack on the Speaker of the Parliament, Mohamed Nasheed, the former President of Maldives, as an act of terrorism and officials said that extremists were responsible for the violence. Mr Nasheed had earned a reputation as "an outspoken critic of religious extremism", which is seen to put non-Muslims including Christians at risk.[283]

July 2021 The Maldives Customs Service declared that it was joining forces with the police to investigate alleged incidents of Christian literature being mailed from abroad to individuals, companies and institutions in the country. The authorities were unable to verify the claims, and the investigation was closed before the end of the year.[284]

June 2022 The US State Department's Religious Freedom Report highlighted ongoing problems for Christians in the Maldives. The document cites reports stating that conversion to Christianity "easily result[s] in [individuals] being reported to Muslim leaders or authorities". Expatriate Christians, a majority of whom have travelled from India and Sri Lanka to work in tourism, are described as being "'closely watched'".[285]

MALI

Like many countries in the Sahel region of Africa, Mali has suffered from the consequences of the attempts by Islamist extremists to establish a caliphate in the area. The government and the constitution are moderately Islamic, but there are many stipulations for freedom of religion, e.g. the constitution prohibits religious discrimination and grants individual freedom of religion in conformity with the law. However, non-state actors are persecuting Christians in the country. After the *coup d'état* in August 2020, the transitional government adopted the Transition Charter, recognising the validity of the 1992 constitution's definition of the country as secular and prohibiting religious discrimination.[286]

Sunni Muslims make up most of the 18 million followers of Islam in Mali.[287] Of 466,900 Christians in the country, two-thirds are Catholic and one-third Protestant.[288] In 2012, radical Islamist groups seized control of the north of Mali, driving Christians from their homes.[289] This displacement still affects Christians, although many have returned to their homes under police protection. Muslim converts to Christianity can face violent coercion from relatives and members of their community.[290] Jama'at Nasr al-Islam wal-Muslimin

Population
20.3 million

Religions
Muslims	88.75%
Ethno-religionists	8.75%
Christians	2.25%
Others	0.25%

Christian Population
466,900

(JNIM), a US-designated terrorist group, have kidnapped Christians, including Swiss Christian missionary Beatrice Stoeckli, who was eventually killed, and Colombian Sister Gloria Cecilia Narváez.[291]

The jihadists have begun to overrun areas in central Mali, further adding to the instability. On 3rd December 2021, there was an attack in the Bandiagara region that killed at least 32 persons.[292] According to the priest of Barapreli Church in the Bandiagara area, terrorist and other armed groups continued to ban Catholicism, and instead taught Islam, imposing *Shari'a* on Catholics. He added that they have forced the local Christian community in Didja near the church to learn the *Qu'ran* and perform prayers as prescribed by Islam. Conversely, Caritas said most Catholic churches in the country remained open.[293]

In some areas, representatives of Caritas stated that extremist groups were banning alcohol and pork, and forcing women of all faiths in parts of the region of Mopti to wear veils.[294] JNIM attacked multiple towns in Mopti, threatening Christian, Muslim, and traditional religious communities in the process.[295] In some areas controlled by Islamists rather than the Malian government, Christians are denied resources and not given land and water to grow their crops.[296]

Christian missionaries expressed concern about the rise of extremist groups in remote areas of the country. Protestant leaders highlighted a Christian teacher who was forced to flee his home after terrorists and armed groups threatened him in Mandiakoy village in Ségou Region.[297]

As is often the case with Islamist aggression, Christian women in Mali face the threat of abduction and forced marriage.[298] Female converts to Christianity are vulnerable to killings, physical violence, and sexual abuse.[299] Men, on the other hand, are at risk of kidnapping and forced recruitment into jihadists groups.[300] It is common for jihadists to weaken Christian families and communities by targeted attacks on homes and businesses. Christian converts are rejected socially and have reduced access to jobs or education.

October 2020 Christian missionary Beatrice Stoeckli was killed by Islamist group Jama'at Nasr al-Islam wal Muslimin (JNIM), according to the Swiss Ministry of Foreign Affairs.[301] She was first kidnapped in April 2012, but later released. She was seized again in 2016 while working in Timbuktu.[302] Ignazio Cassis, the Head of the Federal Department of Foreign Affairs in Switzerland, said: "It is with great sadness that I learned of the death of our fellow citizen. I condemn this cruel act and express my deepest sympathies to the relatives."[303]

June 2021 Five Christians in Mali were abducted, including a Catholic priest.[304] 72 hours after being kidnapped, Father Leon Douyon was released, along with the other abductees. Major Abass Dembélé, the governor of the Mopti region, central Mali, revealed that the five were released following the breakdown of the kidnappers' vehicle near Mali's border with Burkina Faso. He said: "The kidnappers therefore decided to abandon the vehicle somewhere in the bush and, thanks to the mediation of local Dogon and Fulani notables, they agreed to free their five hostages, who had become very cumbersome."[305]

October 2021 Sister Gloria Cecilia Narváez was released after being in jihadist captivity since February 2017. Sister Gloria of the Franciscan Sisters of Mary Immaculate was abducted near the border with Burkina Faso by the militant group JNIM on 7th February 2017 in the village of Karangasso, near Koutiala city in the southerly Sikasso region, where she was ministering to the poor. She later told ACN about her ordeal in captivity. She said she used to pray: "My God, it is hard to be chained and to receive blows, but I live this moment as you present it to me... And in spite of everything, I would not want any of these men [i.e. her captors] to be harmed." She added: "They asked me to repeat bits of Muslim prayers, to wear Islamic-style garments, but I always let it be known that I was born in the Catholic faith, that I grew up in that religion, and that for nothing in the world would I change that, even if it cost me my life."[306]

December 2021 ACN received reports that jihadists in the Ségou region were stepping up efforts to seize swathes of land and to establish *Shari'a* law in the territory under their control. A local source told ACN that Katiba Macina, an Islamist group with links to Al Qaeda in the Islamic Maghreb, burnt rice fields and attacked farmers attempting to harvest crops. According to the source – which ACN cannot name for security reasons – Katiba Macina have been trying to intimidate the local populace into joining the militants or abandoning their land, so the Islamist extremists can take it. The source said: "The desire to impose Islamic *Shari'a* law is proof that the jihadists, especially those of the Katiba Macina, are working for the expansion of a radical Islam of a kind that many other Muslims do not share". The source added: "The jihadists are acting in the name of religion. Everything that does not conform to their own ideology suffers as a result. That is why there are so many refugees".[307]

MOZAMBIQUE

An Islamist insurgency in Mozambique, waged since 2017, has reportedly claimed the lives of more than 4,000 people[308] and led to the displacement of at least 784,000.[309] The group, known locally as Al Sunnah wa Jama'ah (ASWJ) or Al-Shabab – not to be confused with Al-Shabab in Kenya and Somalia – is affiliated with Daesh (ISIS). Alongside many Muslims, Christians have fallen foul of this violence and have been the victims of direct attacks.

Just before the reporting period, a spate of jihadist attacks saw churches targeted during Holy Week of 2020, signalling the jeopardy Christians in the country face. Bishop Luiz Fernando Lisboa, then of Pemba, Cabo Delgado, told ACN: "Seven small towns or villages were attacked in fact during the days of Holy Week, among others that of Muambula where the Catholic mission of the Sacred Heart of Jesus is situated, in Nangololo. They attacked the church and burnt the benches and a statue of Our Lady, made of ebony. They also destroyed an image of the Sacred Heart of Jesus, to whom the parish is dedicated... They had already attacked and burnt five or six local chapels, but they also burned some mosques. Although ultimately, it seems, the target is the Christian churches."[310]

The jihadists seized the port town of Palma in March 2021, which is close to a Total gas facility.[311] Some reports said up to 150 insurgents attacked the town, leading to the "assassination of hundreds of defenceless people", according to Omar Saranga, a spokesman for the country's

POPULATION
32.25 million

CHRISTIAN POPULATION
17.4 million

RELIGIONS
Christians 54%   Ethno-religionists 28%
Muslims 17.5%   Others 0.5%

defence and security forces.[312] Daesh, on their Telegram channel, boasted on 29th March 2021 that "the caliphate's soldiers seize[d] the strategic town of Palma".[313] Further, Amaq, a news agency affiliated to the Islamist group, said the attack "resulted in the deaths of 55 Mozambican forces and Christians including contractors from outside the country".[314] The exodus this attack engendered led to a Catholic priest, Father Antonio Chamboco, telling ACN he was terrified about the fate of his parishioners as "almost nothing is known about their whereabouts".[315]

There have been additional reports of churches being attacked by insurgents.[316] On top of that, over a thousand girls have been kidnapped, including Christians who were forced to either convert to Islam or become slaves *(see June 2021)*.[317]

The latter part of 2021 saw the conflict slow down somewhat, which could be partly explained by the introduction in the northernmost province of Cabo Delgado of forces from Rwanda and member countries of the Southern African Development Community.[318] Also, November to April is the rainy season in Mozambique, when fighting historically slows down. Despite this, the number of attacks began to increase again from the beginning of 2022.[319] January 2022 saw Daesh claim responsibility for a number of assaults in Mozambique, including the torching of villages and the murder of faithful. In the month of June alone, 17,000 people were forced to flee Cabo Delgado province due to terror attacks.[320]

January 2021 A woman watched her husband and brother being killed by terrorists because of their faith, as well as seeing her sisters kidnapped by the jihadists. As a result, she is now looking after 14 children, including her own and those of her brother and sisters. The woman said: "I saw them tie up my husband's hands and torture him shouting 'Allahu Akubar! Allahu Akubar!' before they cut his throat. I saw them kill my brother and some other men in the same way. Then finally they left, taking with them my sisters and some other women. I have not heard from any of them since. I do not know if they are alive or dead."[321]

May 2021 A report by *Observatorio do Meio Rural*, found that more than 1,000 girls had been abducted by the jihadists. Most of the girls were Muslim, but those who were Christian were given a "choice": convert to Islam or become a slave. One of the girls, who escaped the jihadists and did not want to be named, said: "[F]or those who were Christians, and who didn't want to convert…[they] would be chosen by the soldiers to be slaves."

July 2021 A catechist in Mozambique described how he risked his life to save vital Church documents from advancing insurgents, who desecrated, looted and set fire to his parish. Speaking to ACN, Paulo Agostinho, catechist at St Benedict's in Palma, explained that when he returned to his parish after escaping following the attack, the church had been ransacked. He said: "I went back to the parish to see how things were… They took the money, a plasma TV, and even the motorcycle…" Mr Agostinho added that the door was smashed and the terrorists had set fire to sacred images, statues, benches, loudspeakers and even new windows.

August 2021 A captured Christian man risked his life by refusing to convert to Islam. He was allowed to go home, although those who refuse to convert are usually "slaughtered on the spot". Father Kwiriwi Fonseca, who works in Pemba Diocese, told ACN: "We met a Christian who was told 'Do you want to stay here and become Muslim or do you want to go home?' It's risky as some of the people who say they want to go home are slaughtered on the spot." The priest added: "He knew he would be killed but he said it is better to go home. The men decided he could go home, it's very mysterious."[322]

August 2021 A priest revealed that two nuns had been kidnapped by terrorists in Mozambique. Father Kwiriwi Fonseca told ACN: "[We] have experienced two Sisters being kidnapped in the bush. The Sisters were not forced to convert to Islam."

January 2022 Between 3rd and 7th January, Daesh claimed responsibility for seven attacks against Mozambique's Christians. On January 13th, the group claimed responsibility for an attack on the village of Cilate, home to both Christians and Muslims, in the Meluco area of Cabo Delgado, that saw Daesh fighters set fire to 60 homes. The day after that, the village of Pitolha, also containing Christians and Muslims, in the Meluco area, had 20 homes set alight. A pro-Daesh Telegram channel reported on an attack in Limwalamwala Village in Nangade District in Cabo Delgado, killing at least five people and burning 200 houses to the ground.[323]

March 2022 Terrorists attacked an army camp in the Christian town of Nova Zambezia, in Macomia district in north-east Mozambique.[324] Daesh fighters set fire to the homes of Christians and one soldier was killed.

June 2022 Terrorists attacked parishes, displacing priests, as part of a major assault on Cabo Delgado's Ancuabe and Chiure districts, causing 17,000 people to flee Cabo Delgado in June alone. Bishop Antonio Juliasse Sandramo of Pemba told ACN: "We have parishes that have been practically destroyed, priests who are living in difficult situations because they had to abandon their missions empty-handed – children, elderly people and others are in great need, and we can't handle it by ourselves."[325]

September 2022 Terrorists shot dead an 83-year-old Sister Maria de Coppi during an attack on a Catholic compound in Chipene, Nacala Diocese on Tuesday 6th. Bishop Alberto Vera told ACN, attackers "broke open the tabernacle and vandalised part of the sacristy". The jihadists also torched the church, school, health centre, library, boys' and girls' boarding schools, vehicles, and the priests' and nuns' houses.[326]

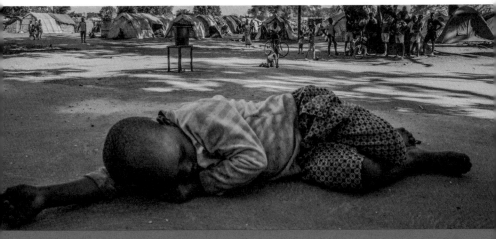

NIGERIA

More than 7,600 Christians were killed, and 5,200 Christians abducted between January 2021 and June 2022, according to one analysis. 2021 also witnessed attacks on more than 400 churches or Christian institutions.[327] When in November 2021 the United States government removed Nigeria from its list of 'Countries of Particular Concern' in matters of religious freedom, the Christian Association of Nigeria's president Rev'd Samson Ayokunle said there was a militant Islamist agenda to "wipe away Christianity", highlighting both the problems caused by Islamist groups trying to carve out a caliphate in the north-east and armed attacks on Christian communities in the Middle Belt. Rev'd Ayokunle went on to draw attention to other problems, including state discrimination, accusing many northern states of preventing church construction, and recent kidnappings.[328]

While all communities in the north-east have suffered at the hands of Boko Haram in its various iterations, the jihadists' ideological opposition to Christianity was made clear in a 2012 video message in which they publicly declared a "war on Christians". In 2015 they pledged loyalty to Daesh (ISIS) and were formally renamed Islamic State: West Africa Province (ISWAP). This led to a schism in August 2016, when Daesh replaced ISWAP leader Abubakar Shekau with Abu Musab Al-Barnawi. Shekau refused to accept the move, leading to a *de facto* schism. After running battles in Sambisa Forest, Abubaker Shekau's forces were decimated, and he is reported to have committed suicide in May 2021. Following this, there were a number of surrenders: e.g. in August 2021, 67 adult male fighters were part of a group of 186 who surrendered.

RELIGIONS
Christians 46.25%   Muslims 46.25%
Traditional 7.25%   Others 0.25%

Boko Haram have raided civilian settlements, abducting numerous individuals, mostly girls and young women, often forcing them to marry their members. Up to 95 percent of those abducted and forced to marry are Christians, and this is accompanied by coercion to convert to Islam, and compulsion to enter sexual relations.[329] The jihadists released videos of Christians being beheaded in both December 2020 and May 2022 – the five executed in 2020 were part of a group kidnapped on Christmas Day. Boko Haram's activities have significantly contributed to the figure of 75,644 Nigerians killed over the last 13 years – of which roughly 60 percent were Christians and 40 percent were Muslims.[330]

Dating back to the 1970s, there was conflict with members of the Muslim-majority nomadic Fulani herder community, as circumstances such as loss of traditional grazing lands drove them further south in search of new pastures. Clashes occurred as their cattle grazed on arable land owned by farmers, mostly belonging to the Christian community. However, it should be stressed that these clashes were not intrinsically religious in nature. While many of the narratives seeking to explain the violence in the Middle Belt over the last decade still rely on the farmer-herder clashes as the primary frame in which to understand the issue, this is a naïve and overly simplistic interpretation of a situation that has grown and transformed from its root causes. Speaking to ACN in June 2022, Archbishop Matthew Man-Oso Ndagoso of Kaduna said "[I]n the last 10 years it has taken a different dimension also. The herdsmen used to be armed with sticks and bows, now they have AK47s".[331] The UK All-Party Parliamentary Group for International Freedom of Religion or Belief has noted that "Church attacks do seem to illustrate that there is a religious dimension to the violence".[332] Such attacks would include the June 2022 targeting of Evangelical and Catholic churches in Southern Kaduna *(see June 2022 below)*. In Nigeria these attacks are often referred to as "Bandit" attacks, denoting that this is a distinct phenomenon from the old farmer-herder conflicts. A number of factors, including political dissatisfaction and poverty from an inability to make a living from cattle rearing, have pushed members of the Fulani herder community to criminal activity to support themselves. There is growing evidence that Bandit groups are working with Boko Haram, suggesting that at least some of these groups have become radicalised.[333] Radicalisation would account for the regular Bandit attacks on Christian-majority settlements and churches.

During the period under review there were also allegations that police and army officers killed more than 400 Christians from the Igbo ethnic group in the eastern states, in street shootings and custodial killings. According to official narratives, extra-judicial killings involved members of the separatist group IPOB/ESN – which stands accused of killing more than 300 members of the security forces. With narratives and counter-narratives obscuring any attempt to form a clear picture, more research is required to determine the exact nature of these deaths.[334]

December 2020 Professor Richard Solomon Musa Tarfa was released on bail after almost a year in pre-trial detention. The co-founder of the Du Merci Centres – orphanages for Christian children – was detained by authorities on 25th December 2019, after armed police officers raided the centre in Kano State without a warrant. On 31st December the centre in adjoining Kaduna State was also raided, and later demolished by the state government. The Christian children were transferred to the state-run Nasarawa Children's Home. They complained of not being allowed to attend school or church, and of maltreatment because of their faith. Professor Tarfa was originally told he was being charged with operating an orphanage illegally, but this was changed to "criminal abduction of minors" after documents were produced showing the orphanages were properly registered.[335]

December 2020 Father Valentine Ezeagu was kidnapped by four armed men while driving to his father's funeral in the southern state of Imo on Tuesday 15th. He was released 36 hours later. Father George Okorie, Superior General of the Congregation of the Sons of Mary, Mother of Mercy, said: "When I spoke to Father Valentine, he told me that seeing him saying his Rosary made his abductors confused. They started having a guilty conscience. It made them realise that, dressed in his soutane [priest's cassock], they had not got the right person so they gave him food and released him."[336]

January 2021 Bandits kidnapped and killed Father John Gbakaan Yaji, of Minna Diocese, in Nigeria's Middle Belt region, as he was returning from Mass. His body was discovered on Sunday 17th.[337]

February 2021 Hauwa Halima Maigana, one of the 276 mostly Christian Chibok schoolgirls abducted by Boko Haram from the Government Girls Secondary School in April 2014, managed to escape from her captors.[338]

April 2021 Four women were kidnapped and another parishioner killed during a Bandit attack on Haske Baptist Church in Manini village, Chikun Local Government Area, southern Kaduna State on Sunday 25th.[339]

May 2021 Bandits opened fire on two churches in Kaduna State's Chikun Local Government Area: the Baptist church in Lukuru village and a "White Garment" church near Bakin Kasuwa on Gwagwada Road, early on Wednesday 5th. Two persons were killed instantly during the attacks, others were wounded or kidnapped.[340]

July 2021 More than 120 students were abducted from Bethel Baptist High School during the early hours of Monday 5th. The kidnappers opened fire on security guards at the school in Maramara Chikun District, just outside the state capital Kaduna, seizing most of the boarders. According to the *Guardian*, the attack was at least the fourth school kidnapping in Kaduna State since December.[341]

July 2021 Boko Haram/ISWAP set up check points along the highway from Maiduguri to Damaturu, abducting Christian travellers and letting Muslim ones continue. Kallamu Musa Ali Dikwa, Director General of the Centre for Justice on Religion and Ethnicity, gave Sahara Reporters evidence of the practice: "Just recently, a bus driver was stopped and they asked how many Christians are in the bus, he said two, they picked those two and the rest continued on their journey."[342]

August 2021 More than seven years after being seized by Boko Haram, Chibok schoolgirl Ruth Ngladar Pogu was reunited with her family on Saturday 7th. In captivity the Christian girls were given the stark choice of converting to Islam and marrying Boko Haram fighters or becoming slaves. Like many of the girls, Ruth opted to convert and marry. She was recovered, with her two children, when her Boko Haram husband surrendered to the Nigerian military.[343]

September 2021 Multiple attacks on Christian-majority communities in Kaduna State on Sunday 26th saw 49 people killed in Kaura Local Government

Area, and 27 members of the Evangelical Church Winning All kidnapped, and one parishioner killed, in Gabachuwa community.[344]

October 2021 Christ the King Seminary, near Kafanchan, southern Kaduna, was raided by men who abducted three seminarians on the evening of Monday 11th. Six other seminarians had to be taken to hospital. The students that were kidnapped from their college chapel were released on Wednesday 13th.[345]

December 2021 Boko Haram/ISWAP killed 12 Christians as they were returning home from church services in the Christian-majority Kilangal village, Borno State on Sunday 19th. Christians fled as houses were torched and shops looted.[346]

February 2022 A member of the Christian Association of Nigeria (CAN) was kidnapped when delivering the ransom for the last Bethel Baptist High School student in captivity. The boy, the youngest of those abducted, refused to return. Rev'd Joseph John Hayab, Chairman of CAN in Kaduna State, said: "The Bandits were said to be showering the boy with gifts… thereby, making him reject the offer of freedom."[347]

March 2022 Father Felix Fidson Zakari was among 100 people abducted by Bandits in Kaduna State, as part of night-time attacks on 10 Christian-majority settlements in Giwa County on Thursday 24th. According to witnesses, the pastor of St Ann's Catholic Church was identified and taken away at gun point. Around 50 people were killed: women and children were among the dead.[348]

April 2022 Father Joseph Akete Bako was reportedly tortured to death by his kidnappers, sometime between 18th and 20th. He was abducted from St John's Catholic Church, Kudenda, Kaduna State, where he was parish priest, on 8th March 2022.[349]

May 2022 Deborah Emmanuel died after being stoned and set on fire by fellow students at the Shehu Shagari College of Education in Sokoto, north-western Nigeria for having sent messages allegedly insulting the Islamic religion to a WhatsApp group during the holidays. She was attacked when she returned for the new school term. Riots broke out in Sokoto after two students, Bilyaminu Aliyu and Aminu Hukunci, were arrested for her murder. Churches were attacked throughout the state capital.[350]

May 2022 A video showing 20 Nigerian Christians being executed by Boko Haram/ISWAP was released on Thursday 12th. One of the terrorists stated that the executions were revenge for the killing of Daesh leader Abu Ibrahim Al-Hashimi Al-Qurashi in Syria by US Special Forces.[351]

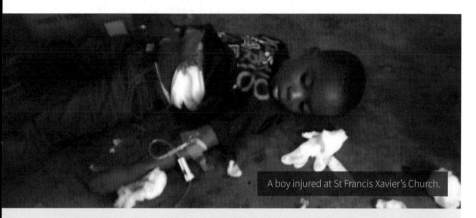
A boy injured at St Francis Xavier's Church.

June 2022 At least 40 people, including children, were killed when armed men fired randomly into the congregation at St Francis Xavier's Catholic Church in Owo, Ondo State on Pentecost Sunday (5th June). This was the first church attack in the state in south-west Nigeria. Father Augustine Ikwu told ACN: "The identity of the perpetrators remains unknown while the situation has left the community devastated."[352]

June 2022 Two major attacks occurred within a fortnight in Kajuru Local Government Area, Southern Kaduna. On Sunday 5th buildings belonging to the Evangelical Church Winning All were razed in Dogo Noma and Maikori villages, and 32 persons were reported dead after attacks on four villages near Maro. Bandits arrived on c. 150 motorcycles, each carrying three men armed with AK-47s. A helicopter also carried out air strikes.[353] On Sunday 19th three were killed when Bandits opened fire in St Moses' Catholic Church, Robuh at the end of Mass. Others were abducted. There were four other attacks the same day and no fewer than 36 were taken.[354]

September 2022 Rev'd Bung Fon Dong was abducted at gunpoint from his home in Ganawuri, Plateau State at c.10pm on Sunday 11th. His wife was shot and injured, and Church security guard James Ngyang was killed during the kidnapping. Bandits from the Fulani community were suspected. A ransom of ₦20 million (£40,500) was demanded.[355]

Nigeria

Searching for a Future

Catherine Ibrahim with her children Daniel and Salome in an IDP camp run by the Catholic Diocese of Maiduguri, Borno State. Catherine told ACN how Boko Haram seized her and murdered her husband. She was reunited with her children in March 2017.

Fr Fidelis helping the women and orphans.

Most of the survivors of extremist violence being cared for by the Human Resource and Skill Acquisition Centre in Maiduguri are women. They have all undergone terrible ordeals: some have witnessed the murder of their husbands; others were sexually abused; some were even ordered to act as suicide bombers. All of these ordeals have left their mark on them, and the women show signs of exhaustion, depression and post-traumatic stress.

With local authorities having done little to address their practical and psychological needs, the Church stepped in.

Victims of Boko Haram are cared for and rehabilitated, and experts including psychologists help them to come to terms with their experiences. Programmes last between six months and two years, depending on their needs.

They are also taught a profession, so that they will have a life after captivity, and women have become seamstresses, shoemakers, bakers and caterers. This enables widows to care for themselves and their families.

Fr Joseph Fidelis who runs the centre said: "Thank you Aid to the Church in Need for the support you have given us… We need your help [so] that we may support these people who are suffering."

NORTH KOREA

North Korea has one of the world's worst human rights records and consistently emerges as the country where Christians suffer the most, experiencing "extreme persecution".[356] However, any definitive categorisation of the scale of religious freedom violations is made problematic by lack of independent access to a country which is secretive and closed to the outside world.[357]

Nonetheless, first-hand witness testimony of systematic brutal targeting of people of religious faith, especially Christians, demonstrates the state's absolute refusal to honour its constitutional commitment to religious freedom. Few, if any, of those punished are likely to be guilty of the constitution's stipulation that "religion must not be used as a pretext for drawing in foreign forces for harming the state or social order".[358] Against the backdrop of some of the harshest treatment of religious groups, the government continues to articulate its religious freedom credentials. For example, a 2014 official government document states: "Freedom of religion is allowed and provided by the State law within the limit necessary for securing social order, health, social security, morality and other human rights."[359]

North Korea's Songbun system categorises citizens according to their loyalty to the state. Religious believers are automatically classed as "hostile" and "subjected to severe repression".[360]

RELIGIONS
Agnostics 58%   Atheists 15.5%   Neo-religionists 12.5%
Ethno-religionists 12%   Buddhists 1.5%   Christians 0.5%

While all religious groups suffer, evidence indicates that Christians experience what Christian persecution charity Open Doors calls the "most extreme" persecution.[361] This is the case in spite of "government attempts to provide an illusion of religious freedom to the outside world through state-backed religious organisations and sites such as Jangchong Cathedral".[362] Some reports suggest that Christianity is the most persecuted faith group in the country because of the religion's perceived links with the West.[363] The 2021 report by the UK All-Party Parliamentary Group (APPG) on North Korea concluded that anti-Christian atrocities "reach the threshold of genocide".[364] The APPG's inquiry found evidence of government officials being involved in murder and killings, torture, inhuman and degrading treatment or punishment, forced abortions and infanticide as well as modern-day slavery.[365]

Describing state attacks on Christians as "systematic", advocacy organisation Korea Future declared that under Kim Jong-un the persecution "has been purposely directed at the destruction of Christian communities". In 2021 the organisation issued a second volume of its report into persecution, drawing on 456 documented cases of human rights violations involving 244 victims and 141 perpetrators. The report found that Christians were among those who "experienced arbitrary arrest and detention, forced labour, torture and cruel, inhuman treatment, the denial of fair trial, the denial to the right of life and sexual violence."[366]

The US Commission on International Religious Freedom's 2022 report on North Korea stated that for most Christians collective worship is impossible because of "pervasive surveillance and severe repression". It adds that owning a Bible "is considered extremely risky and life-threatening if discovered" and that the punishment for religious practice includes "summary execution".[367] It is estimated that between 50,000 and 70,000 citizens were jailed for being Christian. UK-based religious freedom organisation CSW calculated that 200,000 individuals were in prison camps, many for being Christian.[368] The regime continues to produce propaganda promoting hatred towards Christians. One report described anti-Christian rhetoric in schools, in which children are told that Christian missionaries are spies of countries "who seek opportunities to invade North Korea". It went on to describe "graphic images of missionaries" who were portrayed as vampires preying on children.[369]

October 2020 Korea Future, a human rights advocacy organisation, issued a dossier detailing persecution against Christians in the country, drawing on interviews with 117 survivors, witnesses and perpetrators, collected over a period of seven months. The research identified 273 victims of religious oppression, of whom 215 were Christians ranging in age from three to more than 80. Nearly 60 percent of victims were women and girls. The charges against them included possession of religious articles, contact with known religious individuals, attending places of worship and discussing religious belief. Punishments included arrest, detention, imprisonment, interrogation, torture, sexual violence and public trials.[370]

June 2021 The government destroyed the inter-Korean liaison office, in Kaesong, close to the South Korean border. According to media reports, the building was demolished in response to defectors in South Korea sending anti-North Korean government literature over the border. Reports from Christian media stated that the material had from time to time included Christian literature, such as first-hand witness statements written by North Korean Christian refugees, Bibles and digital copies of Christian sacred texts on memory sticks (flash drives).[371]

July 2021 The UK All-Party Parliamentary Working Group on North Korea released the findings of its *Inquiry into Human Rights Violations in North Korea 2014-2020/21*. The inquiry cited evidence of North Korea state officials carrying out murders, torture, sexual violence, sex trafficking, slavery, forced abortions and infanticide, and concluded that crimes directed against Christians "reached the threshold of genocide". The report, which involved APPG members Fiona Bruce MP and Lord Alton of Liverpool, concluded: "The atrocities amount to crimes against humanity."[372]

December 2021 Korea Future Initiative's report *Religious Women as Beacons of Resistance in North Korea* was published, giving witness testimonies, including those of Christian women. Of a sample size of 151, the report found violations suffered by Christian women included 140 cases of arbitrary deprivation of liberty, five cases of forced labour, 33 cases of torture and cruel, inhuman or degrading treatment, one case of sexual violence including rape and 11 cases of refoulement.[373]

February 2022 A group of Christians were sent to a remote village to carry out hard labour after being found in possession of a Bible. One of them sent a letter describing what happened. She wrote: "When our Bible was found, it was immediately destroyed. And because we are Christians we were exiled to a remote village with no chance of ever leaving. Work here is hard. Rations are limited. We are always hungry or sick."[374]

June 2022 The Catholic Bishops' Conference of Korea (CBCK) held a ceremony marking the end of research into the cause of beatification of Bishop of Pyongyang Francis Hong Yong-ho and 80 others killed by the Communists during the Korean War. Bishop Yong-ho was jailed in 1949 before disappearing, as did 49 other priests, seven male religious and 25 lay people. Before the papers were sent to the Congregations for the Causes of Saints in Rome, CBCK President Bishop Mathias Ri Iong-hoon of Suwon said: "In the harsh reality of a still-divided country in which the separation between North and South and ideological conflicts continue today, I sincerely hope that the promotion of the beatification of these martyrs will serve as a foundation for reconciliation and unity."[375]

PAKISTAN

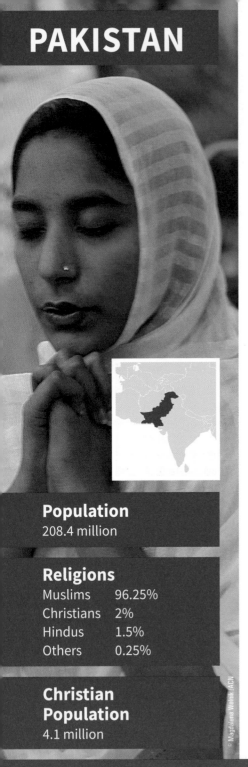

© Magdalena Wolnik/ACN

Population
208.4 million

Religions
Muslims	96.25%
Christians	2%
Hindus	1.5%
Others	0.25%

Christian Population
4.1 million

The tightening of security at churches in Pakistan in response to the Taliban's return to power in neighbouring Afghanistan in August 2021 was part of a cycle of growing concern for Christians in the region.[376] Across Pakistan, conditions for Christians and other religious minorities "continued their negative trajectory".[377] Although the Pakistan government took steps to protect communities marking religious feasts,[378] the impact of other policies, legislation and cultural prejudices caused an overall decline in the rights of Christians. High profile cases of vulnerable Christians falsely accused, including teenage Maira Shahbaz,[379] living in hiding for alleged apostasy, and nurse Tabitha Gill,[380] accused of blasphemy by her colleagues, demonstrated that minorities going about their daily lives ran an increased risk of harassment, arrest or violence. These cases also showed that law enforcement agencies and court justices were frequently prejudiced against them, with judges, magistrates and others influenced by mobs and threats.

In July 2022 Archbishop Sebastian Shaw of Lahore told ACN that action was needed – including from the West – to tackle the kidnapping, sexual assault and forced conversion of young people.[381] The previous November, ACN launched its *Hear Her Cries* report which documented abduction cases, such as that of Farah Shaheen *(see February 2021 below)*, and categorised

Pakistan as one of the worst offenders worldwide of gender specific religious persecution.[382] It cited evidence showing that in just one province – Sindh – there were in one year alone (2018) more than 1,000 cases involving Christian and Hindu women suffering forced conversion.[383] The continuous stream of reports of individuals from religious minority backgrounds suffering various forms of abuse showed how far the authorities were falling short of the constitution's requirement that "adequate provision shall be made for the minorities to freely profess and practise their religions and develop their cultures".[384] Although security measures were stepped up at festivals including Christmas and Easter,[385] a culture of impunity persisted with frequent reports of "targeted killings, lynching, mob violence… desecration of houses of worship and cemeteries."[386] Lower-caste Christians reported being forcibly evicted from their homes amid allegations that government officials were colluding with individuals seeking to expropriate their land.[387] The South Asia Terrorism Portal reported that sectarian attacks and killings by armed groups had increased.[388]

By law, at least five percent of government posts, both federal and provincial, are to be allocated to Christians and other minorities.[389] However, the Supreme Court criticised the government for failing to implement the five percent quota so that across the country more than 30,000 such posts remained unoccupied.[390]

Lack of political representation may explain the continued failure to effectively tackle abuse of Pakistan's controversial Blasphemy laws, which affected Christians and other minorities. The legislation includes sections 295b and 295c which respectively impose life imprisonment for desecrating Quranic texts and the death sentence for disrespecting the Islamic Prophet Mohammad.[391] Research showed a disproportionately high number of blasphemy cases involving Christians: of the 1,550 people accused of blasphemy between 1986 and 2017, Christians numbered 238 (15.3 percent) even though they make up less than two percent of the population. By contrast Muslims who are 96.4 percent of the populace made up only 46.5 percent of cases, a total of 720.[392] Accusations against Christians frequently resulted in "lynching, mob attacks on entire neighbourhoods and extra-judicial killings".[393] Although the number of blasphemy cases was reportedly down in 2021 as compared with 2020,[394] legislation passed during this period suggested a stiffening of resolve to clamp down on acts of disrespect to Islam. The Punjab Provincial Assembly passed a bill banning printed material deemed offensive to the Prophet of Islam and demanding that people always refer to him using titles including "the Last Prophet of God".[395]

In the field of education too, evidence suggested a large number of blasphemy allegations and violent acts against minorities. Evidence showed that in school curricula there were "factual inaccuracies, historical revisionism and easily recognisable omissions [which] reinforce negative stereotypes and create a narrative of conflict towards religious minorities."[396]

January 2021 Christian nurse Tabitha Gill, 30, was attacked and beaten by staff at Sobhraj Maternity Hospital in Karachi after a Muslim colleague falsely accused her of blasphemy. She was accused of making derogatory remarks against the Muslim Prophet Mohammad and other prophets in contravention of Section 295c of the Pakistan Penal Code. There were claims that she had been tied up by an angry mob, tortured and locked inside a room before being taken to the police station. Ms Gill, who was a senior nurse and who had worked at the hospital for nine years, was initially released but, after a crowd gathered in front of the police station, she was arrested again and charged.[397]

February 2021 Faisalabad District and Sessions Court declared that 12-year-old Christian girl Farah Shaheen's forced marriage to Khizar Ahmed Hayat, a man more than 30 years her senior, was invalid. Farah had been abducted from her home in June 2020. Her father Asif Masih said police insulted him when he tried to report the case. In December 2020, they discovered Farah in her abductor's home, tethered to a rope, her feet shackled and so distressed she was unable to speak. An official birth certificate showed Farah was aged 12 but medics investigating her age at the request of the courts gave it as 16 or 17. Finally the court ruled that the marriage was not binding as it had not been registered with the local authorities and Farah was allowed to return to her father and the rest of her family.[398]

May 2021 Hundreds of Muslims were accused of attacking a Christian village in Chak 5 in Okara, Punjab Province after a quarrel between young Christians cleaning the entrance to their church and a Muslim passer-by. Christian men and women were beaten with iron bars, houses were broken into and belongings stolen or broken. The violence erupted after the passer-by, Muhammad Khalil, accused the young Christian cleaners of soiling his suit with dust and water.[399]

December 2021 Sindh High Court gave custody of 14-year-old Christian Arzoo Raja, abducted, forcibly married and converted to Islam, back to her parents but only on condition that she remain Muslim. The girl's abductor, aged 33, and the cleric who conducted their so-called marriage and the girl's alleged conversion to Islam maintained their innocence. They said Arzoo had reached the age of consent according to *Shari'a* law.[400]

January 2022 Police arrested Christian man Rehmat Masih, accusing him of desecrating pages of the *Qur'an*. Mr Masih, 44, had worked for 20 years at Zam Zam publishers, responsible for printing and binding copies of the Islamic holy book. One day at work, some Quranic texts were discovered in a sewage drain and Mr Masih was accused of ripping them out of a book and putting them down the drain. In court, Mr Masih was charged with an offence under Section 295b of Pakistan's Penal Code, which carries a sentence of life for desecrating the *Qur'an*.[401]

January 2022 Tributes were paid to Christian pastor William Silraj who was killed by gunmen on motorbikes who struck as he was driving away from a Sunday service at a church in Peshawar. The pastor was shot in the head and the chest. Alongside him in the car was the Reverend Patrick Naeem, priest-in-charge of the Church of Pakistan parish, who was rushed to hospital with gun wounds. Nobody claimed responsibility, but extremist group Tehreek-e-Taliban Pakistan (TTP) was suspected of carrying out the attack.[402]

May 2022 Catholic woman Shagufta Kausar, held for seven years on death row for alleged blasphemy, said that, despite torture and blackmail, she refused to deny her Christian beliefs. Shagufta was arrested in July 2013 with her husband, Shafqat Masih for allegedly sending offensive texts about the Muslim Prophet Mohammad. She said: "In jail, we were tortured. The officers told my husband that if he did not confess, they would rape me in front of him, and so he confessed, even though we were both innocent. We were in jail for eight months before a judge found us guilty and sentenced us to death." She explained that she was frequently told that if she converted to Islam she would eventually be released. After the couple were acquitted by Lahore High Court in June 2021, she praised organisations including ACN for helping them find justice and be reunited with their young children.[403]

June 2022 A close relation of Christian girl Maira Shahbaz reported that he was continuing to encounter suspicious men determined to hunt her down. By then Maira had spent 18 months living in hiding in one room with her siblings and mother after being accused of apostasy. Maira's suffering began in April 2020 when, aged 14, she was abducted by Mohamad Nakash Tariq, who was accused of raping her and forcing her to marry him and convert.[404] In spite of a birth certificate proving she was underage, he convinced Lahore High Court that they were legally wed despite the imam cited in the marriage certificate disputing its legitimacy. Maira subsequently escaped. Since autumn 2020, ACN's UK office has appealed to the UK government to grant Maira asylum, with repeated questions in the Westminster Parliament and several meetings with former Home Secretary Priti Patel.[405]

June 2022 Christian farm labourer Younis Masih, 50, from Muslimania village, near Sialkot was killed by men who hacked him to death with scythes. After assailants threw bricks at his head, his son, Abdul, said it was so disfigured he could not recognise him. According to police, his attackers put a hosepipe round his neck and dragged the body, dumping it in the street outside his home. Police arrested two Muslim men who owned neighbouring farms next to where Mr Masih worked.[406]

July 2022 Archbishop Sebastian Shaw of Lahore appealed to the international community to take more action to prevent the abduction, sexual assault and forced conversion of young people from Christian and other minority backgrounds in Pakistan. Speaking at an ACN event in Portugal, he said nowhere in Pakistan could a young person's safety be guaranteed: "These children are not even free to play in the garden. We have a duty to speak about what is happening, to prevent these cases."[407]

July 2022 18-year-old Rimsha Riaz was raped at gunpoint by her employer, local Muslim businessman Haji Ali Akbar, after he summoned her to his office at the end of her work shift on the pretext that she would be offered more work. After the family absented themselves, Mr Akbar went to her family home with four armed men and shouted: "I will kill you if you remain absent tomorrow and make sure you bring the girl." Miss Riaz fainted and was taken to hospital.[408]

July 2022 Lahore High Court sentenced Ashfaq Masih to death by hanging on Monday 4th following his trial for blasphemy. Masih has maintained his innocence since he was accused in June 2017. He claims the accusation was triggered by imam Muhammad Irfan refusing to pay him for motorcycle repairs, claiming his religious status exempted him. Masih replied: "I do not follow anyone other than Jesus and asked to be paid."[409]

August 2022 Christian man Wilson Masih, 65, was shot dead and three teenagers were left injured when three gunmen on motorbikes attacked a Christian colony in the Mashtung area of Baluchistan. Christians protested an hour after the shooting, blocking the national highway. In response to the incident, two police were posted on the gates of the Christian colony. A Muslim-majority town, Mashtung is home to only 115 Christians. Poverty-stricken Baluchistan has suffered a reported increase in Islamist militant attacks on Christians, Hazara Shi'as and other minorities.[410]

Pakistan

Searching for Justice

Aid to the Church in Need is supporting a nationwide programme to help Christian girls and young women all over Pakistan threatened by abduction, sexual abuse, forced marriage and conversion. Teaming up with Catholic-run National Commission for Justice and Peace (NCJP), the initiative to Help and Protect Christian Girls seeks to come to the aid of girls such as Arzoo Raja, Farah Shaheen and Maira Shahbaz, all of whom have been victims of forced conversion and marriage when underage.

The programme includes legal aid, emergency aid, lobbying for legal change and a rights-awareness campaign. One participant in the programme, a 20-year-old woman said it helped her stand strong as they "live in a state of anxiety and constant pressure."

She added: "If we do try to defend our rights, we will be accused of blasphemy or some other charge, based on false accusations, as has already occurred in the past."[411]

Cecil Shane Chaudhry, the NCJP's executive director, told ACN: "We count on you to help us raise a voice against this terrible injustice and help our vulnerable young people."

QATAR

Despite some steps by the authorities to reduce restrictions on religious freedom, Christians and others in Qatar continue to experience oppression. The country has strong traditional ties to Wahhabism and the constitution insists that "Islamic law is the main source of legislation".[412]

Almost all Christians are expatriates and need to register places of worship with the authorities. The development of the Mesaymeer Religious Complex (known as "Church City") near the capital, Doha, provided for the creation of legally approved church buildings.[413] Some "recall a time of closeness when meeting in secret."[414] The Catholic Church of Our Lady of the Rosary was opened in March 2008 and a 15,000-seat-capacity Anglican church was consecrated in September 2013.[415] Plans were developed for other churches to be erected in Mesaymeer and during the period under review it was reported that up to 100,000 Christians were attending services there every week.[416] However, those attending were said to be expatriates, whose churches are "often heavily monitored by the government" but for indigenous Christians "life is much more difficult". According to one report, "a new believer is likely to face extreme pressure from their Muslim family and community if their faith is discovered. Qatar does not officially recognise conversion from Islam, which causes loss of status and legal difficulty concerning property and child custody."[417]

Eight Christian communities have received state registration: Roman Catholics, Maronites, Greek Orthodox, Syriac Orthodox, Coptic Orthodox, Anglicans, Evangelical Protestants and the Inter-Denominational Christian Church (an umbrella group representing several smaller denominations). Only registered communities are granted places of worship. Others are reportedly allowed to practise their faith "privately", but fear arrest.

RELIGIONS
Muslims 79.5%   Christians 13%   Hindus 3%
Agnostics 2%   Buddhists 2%   Others 0.5%

Some, such as the Villa Church Community, have applied repeatedly for registration to the Ministry of Foreign Affairs, without receiving a reply.

In a country where Islam is enshrined in the constitution as the state religion, the law strictly forbids proselytism aimed at Muslims. The law "criminalises proselytising on behalf of an organisation, society or foundation of any religion other than Islam and provides for punishment of up to 10 years in prison".[418] It also bans congregations from advertising religious services – and in the Mesaymeer Religious Complex, crosses, statues and any other Christian symbols which are "visible to the public" are prohibited.

The school curriculum has received criticism from human rights observers for fomenting religious hatred. Government action to combat religious intolerance in official school texts received a mixed reaction from academics and others. A report in the autumn of 2020 by the Institute for Monitoring Peace and Cultural Tolerance in School Education found that, although some texts had been revised, others, notably concerned with Islamic Studies, remained largely unchanged. The report concluded that "Christians are still seen as infidels (kafirun) and [are] expected to go to hell."[419]

Religious freedom observers noted that over the period some house churches were violently forced to close. Others, shut because of the COVID-19 pandemic, were not able to reopen. Societal pressure against non-Muslims is traceable to the influence of Wahhabism. The state-controlled Grand Mosque (Imam Muhammad Ibn. Abdul Wahhab Mosque) in Doha, the largest in the country, has a longstanding Wahhabist tradition. Guest preachers have included Saudi cleric Sa'ad Ateeq Al-Ateeq who reportedly called on Allah to "destroy the Jews and whoever made the Jews and destroy Christians and Alawites and Shiites"[420] during a sermon there. In early 2021 Saudi Arabia, Bahrain and Egypt restored diplomatic ties with Qatar, after severing them for its alleged support for Islamist terrorist groups.[421] Action to improve religious freedom for Christians and other minorities will be a critical litmus test of Qatar's evolving relationship with Wahhabism and other strains of Islamism.

October 2020 Qatar government action against religious intolerance in school textbooks received a mixed reaction from human rights observers reviewing a report by the Institute for Monitoring Peace and Cultural Tolerance in School Education. The report, by IMPACT-se, which studied 238 textbooks between 2016-20, found that although there had been progress in "moderating" the texts, in Islamic religious studies and other sections of the curriculum there was "very little improvement". The report found that although "some anti-Christian material has been removed", "Christians are… expected to go to hell."[422]

October 2021 Author Ahmad Al-Mohannadi wrote a column in the Qatari newspaper Al-Sharq warning against what he alleged were efforts by Christian organisations to "penetrate" Muslim-majority Persian Gulf societies via animated Bible-based missionary cartoons. Al-Mohannadi called for action to stop such videos reaching the Gulf, saying they were harmful to Muslim children.[423]

December 2021 Social media campaigns attacked hotels for putting up Christmas decorations in their lobbies. Some Qatari citizens on social media denounced action marking non-Islamic festivities and warned that the decorations would corrupt young people. Social media influencers posted messages discouraging people from giving festive greetings to non-Muslims at Christmas.[424]

June 2022 The Policy Research Group (POREG) issued a paper claiming that Qatar-based charities "have been bankrolling" organisations which promote international extremism, supporting groups with a track record of attacking Christians and others. UK-based POREG author James Douglas Crikton's report stated: "Millions of dollars [from Qatar charities] have been sent to organisations and individuals promoting Salafi Islam camouflaged as funds for building mosques, madrassas and promoting education and employment opportunities among Muslim communities… Many direct beneficiaries of the Qatar charity funding have in turn been supporting smaller groups which have been associated with global terrorist entities like Al-Qaeda and Islamic State of Iraq and Levant (ISIS). Several of these groups are in fact shell entities, created to hide the real beneficiaries, the Salafi groups."[425]

RUSSIA

Population
144 million

Religions
Christians   82%
Muslims   12.5%
Agnostics   3.75%
Others   1.75%

Christian Population
118 million

Religious groups, including Protestant communities, experienced legal prosecution due to what USCIRF described as "an array of problematic legislation".[426] Numerous prosecutions were brought under Article 5.26 of the Code of Administrative Offences of the Russian Federation during the period under consideration – particularly sections Four ("Russians conducting missionary activity") and Five ("Foreigners conducting missionary activity"). This law was introduced in 2016, as part of the so-called Yarovaya Package of counter-extremism legislation. Despite ostensibly being designed to protect individuals' freedom of conscience and choice of religious confession by preventing aggressive and intrusive proselytism, in effect Article 5.26 goes far further, restricting "missionary activities" including preaching, praying (in certain circumstances), disseminating materials, and providing information about religion outside designated locations, especially in residential premises or public locations. While smaller Evangelical Protestant denominations generally tended to fall foul of these ordinances, in Crimea Christians belonging to the Ukrainian Orthodox Church not in communion with Moscow also suffered under the legislation.

Image: Julia Pashkevich/Pixabay

Russia's 2014 annexation of the Ukrainian part of the Crimean peninsula led to serious violations of human rights for religious groups as Russian laws were introduced into the region.[427] According to the UK's All-Party Parliamentary Group for International Freedom of Religion or Belief: "Since the invasion there have been raids, fines, religious literature seizures, official surveillance, expulsions of invited foreign religious leaders, unilateral cancellation of property rental contracts, and obstructions to regaining Soviet-confiscated places of worship."[428] Ministers also need to hold a Russian passport or a residence permit. Since Crimea came under Moscow's sphere of authority, the autocephalous Ukrainian Orthodox Church has suffered repeated attempts to seize their Cathedral of Sts Vladimir and Olga in Simferopol. In Yevpatoriya, officials ordered the Church to destroy the community's small wooden chapel, claiming it was built illegally. Indeed, Archbishop Kliment of Simferopol and Crimea was arrested in 2019 on charges of terrorism and stealing Church artefacts. Like many religious groups, the Ukrainian Orthodox Church refused to re-register under Russian legislation, as it would mean signing documents which state Crimea is part of the Russian Federation.[429] In 2021, 23 prosecutions were brought under Russian Administrative Code Article 5.26 which led to convictions and fines. Of the 18 whose "crimes" are known, 11 were Christian. Most were Protestant, but one was Ukrainian Orthodox: Archimandrite Damian Skokov *(see August 2021 below)*.[430]

In October 2021 amendments to Russia's Religion Law came into effect requiring new ministers, missionaries and Religious Education teachers trained abroad to receive additional training "in the field of the basics of state-confessional relations". Any group using a religious identifier in its name has to obtain permission from authorities and the list of people banned from leading religious groups was extended.[431]

February 2021 A local congregation affiliated to the Union of Evangelical Christians-Baptists was banned by Anapa city court. The prosecutor stated that from 2018 to 2020, the group evangelised and distributed materials without proper approval from the Ministry of Justice for Krasnodar Krai. The group has regularly held services for up to 200 worshippers, but allegedly refused to register. Their pastor Peter Klimushin was previously fined ₽5,000 in 2018 for illegal missionary activity.[432]

February 2021 A 63-year-old Christian from Kholmsk village, Krasnodar Krai received a 7½ year sentence – the maximum possible – for holding an online Bible study.[433]

March 2021 A member of an Evangelical Baptist Church in Novosergievka, Orenburg Oblast, was charged with conducting illegal missionary activities under Article 5.26. It was alleged that he preached and facilitated the dissemination of religious tracts between 23rd November 2016 and 9th December 2020. Despite denying carrying out missionary activities he was convicted and fined ₽5,000. On 29th December 2020 he had tried to regularise the group's activities with the Ministry of Justice.[434]

April 2021 A minister of the Union of Evangelical Christians-Baptists in Obninsk, Kaluga Oblast was fined for illegal missionary activities under Article 5.26. Pastor Vitaly Glebov's home was visited by FSB (Federal Security Service) agents after several people unknown to him attended a Bible study at his home on 13th January. On Friday 9th April he was found guilty and fined ₽5,000. The pastor said he would appeal.[435]

May 2021 The Bread of Life Church of Christians of Evangelical Faith in Kerch, Crimea, was found guilty of various administrative violations under Article 5.26, which included failing to put their full official name on videos they distributed and on their official social media pages. They were fined ₽30,000.[436]

August 2021 In Crimea, Archimandrite Damian Skokov was fined ₽15,000 on Monday 23rd for having held a service in a monastery. Under Article 5.26 he was charged with illegal missionary activity. His appeal was rejected.[437]

August-September 2021 Local government in Samara ordered the demolition of the Good News Church's place of worship. According to authorities, the church building in Mekhzavod village belonging to the US-planted Pentecostal group violated planning regulations and the change of land usage from residential to religious use was not registered. Pastor Igor Liashevsky insisted that proper permission for construction had been obtained and all violations identified by authorities had been rectified, e.g. the building exceeding the registered height because a 10-foot (three-metre) high cross was subsequently affixed to the top of the building.[438]

March 2022 Russian Orthodox priest Father Ioann Burdin was fined ₽35,000 – roughly one month's average salary – for a Sunday sermon condemning the Russian invasion of Ukraine. The court imposed the fine on the priest from Kostroma Diocese on Thursday 10th March. Father Burdin insisted that the charge was a violation of his religious freedom, saying the court's decision was "a ban not only on expressing one's opinion but also even on professing one's religious beliefs". [439]

March 2022 Sergei Aksyonov, head of the Republic of Crimea, said that he had given instruction for a law to be drafted banning the Orthodox Church of Ukraine.[440]

June-July 2022 A criminal investigation was opened against Father Nikandr Igoryevich Pinchuk for "discrediting" Russia's Armed Forces under part one of Criminal Code Article 280.3, introduced in March 2022. On social media platform Baza, the pastor of St Simeon Verkhotursky's Church in Verkhoturye criticised military action in Ukraine on religious grounds. He told Forum 18: "I am a priest and have the right to denounce evil, regardless of who is involved and the political situation". On Friday 1st July his home was searched. Three memory sticks were removed. He was subsequently questioned at the Investigative Committee's office. In March, Father Pinchuk, who is a priest of the Russian Orthodox Church Abroad (Provisional Supreme Church Authority), was fined ₽35,000 for criticising Russian actions in Ukraine and the shelling of Orthodox churches.[441]

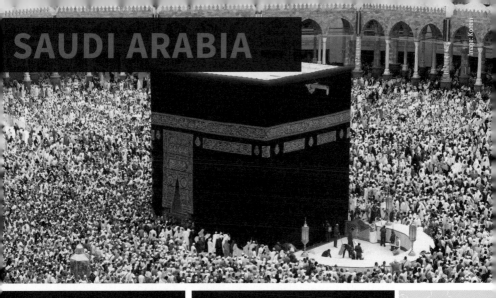

SAUDI ARABIA

POPULATION
35 million

CHRISTIAN POPULATION
2.1 million

RELIGIONS
Muslims 90.5%   Christians 6%   Hindus 2%   Others 1.5%

Severe restrictions on religious liberty mean that Saudi Arabia has one of the world's worst records of intolerance towards Christians and other religious minorities. An unofficial census by the Apostolic Vicariate of Northern Arabia estimates that the country's Catholics number 1.5 million and are made up mainly of foreign workers from India and the Philippines.[442] Some reports indicate a growing number of Saudis identifying as atheists or Christians.[443] However, because of harsh social and legal consequences that result from leaving Islam, they keep quiet about their conversion.[444]

The 1992 Basic Law of Governance states that the country's official religion is Islam and the constitution is the *Qur'an* and the *Sunna*.[445] Non-Islamic places of worship are prohibited, as is public expression of non-Muslim creeds. Importing and distributing non-Islamic religious materials are against the law and proselytism is illegal for both Saudi nationals and foreigners.[446] With a legal system drawn almost exclusively from the Hanbali school of Sunni Islamic jurisprudence, the law forbids "non-Islamic public worship, public display of non-Islamic religious symbols, conversion by a Muslim to another religion and proselytism by a non-Muslim."[447]

But, in practice, Christians and other faith minorities have found ways to manifest their faith discreetly. Expatriate Christians reported that congregations had been able to conduct large Christian worship services in private.[448] This may have resulted from the government limiting the power of the Committee for the Promotion of Virtue and the Prevention of Vice (CPVPV) – a government body responsible for monitoring and reporting moral violations to law enforcement bodies. However, although the CPVPV's wings have been clipped in the last few years, there are reports that it "continues to harass religious minorities."[449]

Christians and others charged with abuse of religious regulations cannot expect mercy at Saudi Arabia's 'Specialised Criminal Court'. The SCC "routinely targets religious minorities and dissidents, imposing egregiously and unduly harsh sentences, denying access to legal counsel, delaying judicial decisions and convicting defendants based partially on confessions obtained through torture".[450]

That said, there have been improvements for Christians and other faith minorities. This stems partly from a slight relaxation in opposition to social changes associated with the West, such as women's empowerment. During the period under review, women were allowed to change their legal names. Although apostasy – conversion from Islam – still carries the death penalty, recently courts have tended to substitute lengthy jail terms.

Signs of change for the better need to be seen in a wider context in which the government has given mixed signals of its intentions regarding a relaxation of the rules. Young people at school continue to be exposed to anti-Christian material. While a number of offensive passages in school textbooks were removed or toned down, the literature still called Christians and other non-Muslims "infidels". [451]

What is clear however is that the government has set its sights on tackling extremist Islam. The Ministry of Islamic Affairs has, for example, increased its vigilance of radical preaching via video surveillance of mosques and closer monitoring of Facebook and Twitter.[452] It remains to be seen whether the action to curb religious extremism will in turn give greater freedoms to Christians or whether it will create a culture of increased distrust in which all but those who follow the approved version of Islam will find themselves more oppressed.

October 2020 There was a commotion on social media after Abdulrahman Al-Sudais, imam of the Grand Mosque of Mecca, gave a homily appealing for dialogue with non-Muslims.[453]

October 2020 Christian leaders were among religious groups represented at a virtual global inter-faith forum which Saudi Arabia held as part of its Presidency of the G20, the premier international economic forum.

November 2020 An attack took place during a First World War remembrance ceremony at the country's only non-Muslim cemetery, which included the detonation of explosives. About 48 hours later, Daesh (ISIS) claimed responsibility for the incident which it said was directed against a number of "consuls of crusading countries" present. The Consul General of France was declared to be the main target because of the publication in France of cartoons depicting the Islamic Prophet Mohammad.[454]

September 2021 A report by the Institute for Monitoring Peace and Cultural Tolerance in School Education (IMPACT-se) concluded that new textbooks in Saudi Arabia showed "significant improvement" as officials altered or removed 22 anti-Christian and anti-Semitic lessons and five lessons about "infidels".[455] However, they noted: "Christians and other non-Muslims are still labelled as infidels throughout."[456]

May 2022 The Muslim World League, reportedly the largest Islamic NGO, organised the Forum on Common Values among Religious Followers in Riyadh. The two-day forum, understood to be the first of its kind, brought together Christian, Jewish, Hindu and Buddhist leaders, as well as Islamic ones, to explore shared values and a common goal for inter-faith cooperation. About 100 religious faith leaders took part in the conference, which, alongside 15 Jewish rabbis, also included Vatican Secretary of State Cardinal Pietro Parolin, Greek Orthodox Patriarch Bartholomew I and Orthodox Archbishop Ivan Zoria from Ukraine. Areas of agreement included the need to respect religious diversity, the importance of inter-faith dialogue and ways to work together to counter extremist ideologies.[457]

September 2022 A Yemeni man was arrested for dedicating his Umrah pilgrimage to Mecca to the late Queen Elizabeth II. Saudi Public Security posted a message on Twitter that the arrest was made for violating Umrah rules after he uploaded a video of himself on pilgrimage with a banner stating: "Umrah for the soul of Queen Elizabeth II, we ask Allah to accept her in heaven and among the righteous."[458] According to Islamic law, Muslims are allowed to perform Umrah for deceased Muslims but not for those of other faiths. Security authorities arrested him for "violating the regulations and instructions" of the holy site.[459]

The 2020 August General Election victory for the Sri Lanka Podujana Peramuna (SLPP) – which stood on a platform of prioritising Sinhalese Buddhist concerns – has strengthened the resurgence of Sinhalese Buddhist nationalism, which initially followed the 2009 victory of the Sri Lankan government in the civil war.[460] This trend has had a negative impact upon minority faith groups in the country, including Christianity, with nationalists voicing strong opposition to people converting from Buddhism, even though it is allowed by law, and to new churches being set up. The activities of minority faiths are often construed as an attack on the country's traditional religious culture and, as the examples below show, even monks have participated in attacks on Christians. Throughout the period under review, there have been reports of authorities either interfering with the activities of churches, or failing to prevent the actions of groups that have attacked Christians, particularly ministers. This especially affects Protestant communities in more rural areas.

Government policies to combat COVID-19 led to infringements of the human rights of minority religious groups and a surge in hate speech against

POPULATION
21 million

CHRISTIAN POPULATION
2 million

RELIGIONS
Buddhists 68%   Hindus 13%   Muslims 9%
Christians 9%   Others 1%

minority faith groups, particularly Muslims. The Church of Ceylon, which is part of the Anglican Communion, said it was "increasingly concerned by the deterioration of human rights in Sri Lanka" and submitted a report to the 48th session of the UN Human Rights Council, warning that state policies were prioritising the Sinhalese Buddhist majority. In particular, it identified forced cremations, which were introduced as a health measure in response to the pandemic, as offending both Christians and Muslims.[461]

The Church of Ceylon report also highlighted the lack of accountability from the government concerning its investigation of the Easter Day 2019 bombings that killed 269 people and injured more than 400. This criticism was repeated by the Catholic Church's Cardinal Malcolm Ranjith, who said official reports had not provided clear answers – but had implicated senior officials. In March 2022 Cardinal Ranjith told ACN:

The Parliament Select Committee report makes recommendations against the former President, former inspector general of police, former defence secretary, former chief of intelligence and other top-level officials, for not having prevented the attacks. They knew beforehand from information they had gathered and also from warnings given by the Indian intelligence services, but they did nothing. In fact, the government seems to have done its best to prevent the arrest of the attackers.[462]

Following the Easter Sunday bombing, the Sri Lankan government banned Thowheeth Jamaath, a local jihadist group allied to Daesh (ISIS). However, no steps were taken to implement the recommendation of the Special Commission of Investigation into the 2019 attacks that Buddhist extremist groups, such as Bodu Bala Sena which had carried out attacks on the Islamic community, be banned for contributing to the radicalisation of parts of the Muslim population.[463]

October 2020 Six police officers entered the Assemblies of God Church, Bakamuna just as the service was ending on Sunday 18th. They took the pastor and a member of the congregation to the police station, where the Officer-in-Charge reproved the pastor for holding services after the village's Buddhist monks had told him to stop. Eight monks attended the meeting. The pastor asked for the demands to be put in writing, and said that if he was breaking the law formal charges should be filed. The Officer-in-Charge refused. Police confiscated a list of church members compiled for COVID-19 contact tracing.[464]

January 2021 Christians were among those challenging a Ministry of Health circular issued in March 2020 requiring mandatory cremation for the bodies of those who died, or were suspected of dying, from COVID-19. Sister Noël Christeen Fernando of the Daughters of Charity of Jesus and Mary, one of the signatories of a petition calling for the rules to be abolished, said: "[O]ur leaders are robbing us of all our rights, from birth to death." Two retired Church of Ceylon bishops, Duleep de Chickera and Kumara Illangasinghe, also signed. Muslims organised numerous protests, as cremation is forbidden in Islam, and there was considerable solidarity with them. While the Catholic Church permits cremation, particularly in times of epidemic, it commends the burial of the body, as do a number of other Christian groups. Cardinal Malcolm Ranjith encouraged Catholics to abide by government policy.[465]

March 2021 Police from the Criminal Investigation Department visited the home of the mother of a pastor from Calvary Church in Padukka on Thursday 18th. She was questioned about her daughter's religious activities and officers asked for contact information for her daughter and her son-in-law.[466]

September 2021: A local official denied Christian burial for a woman from Grama Missionary Church in Karukkamunai's public cemetery, stating that it was a Hindu burial site, so no Christian rites could be performed there. The funeral went ahead as planned on Monday 27th but with a Hindu ceremony.[467]

October 2021 The Catholic Bishops' Conference urged the government to abandon a task force to reform personal laws, headed by nationalist politician and Buddhist monk Galagodaatte Gnanasara of Bodu Bala Sena, expressing fears the project would erode minority rights. No Christians, Hindus or women were appointed to the 13-member "Presidential Task Force for One Country, One Law" set up by President Gotabaya Rajapaksa to consider abolishing personal laws, including the Muslim marriage law and some regional laws that go back several hundred years, and introducing one standardised code.[468]

November 2021 The pastor of Polgolla's Gospel Tabernacle Church was praying with a Christian family at their home on the afternoon of Sunday 20th, when a mob gathered outside, including a Buddhist monk. When the pastor and homeowner went outside to talk to the people, the monk stated it was a "Buddhist village" and the pastor was not welcome. The mob then surrounded another Christian house and began shouting. The pastor and other Christians were assaulted when they tried to stop the mob beating the woman who lived there. They required hospital treatment for their injuries.[469]

March 2022: *c.* 60 Buddhist monks were part of a mob of up to 600 people which entered the grounds of Mercy Gate Chapel in Amalgama on the afternoon of Sunday 6th, and demanded that the community close the building and stop all activities. The pastor was threatened with death if he continued to lead worship. About 20 police officers were present, and told the monks that they needed a legal order to close the chapel. The monks refused to depart, and demanded access to the building's interior. The pastor allowed four monks to enter after being assured that no damage would be done. They questioned the pastor about the chapel's activities and afterwards told the mob that it was not a legitimate church. Everyone left shortly afterwards. Police were investigating, after a complaint was filed against the monks and other mob members for harassment.[470]

SUDAN

Population
43.5 million

Religions
Muslims	91.75%
Christians	4.5%
Ethno-religionists	2.5%
Others	1.25%

Christian Population
2 million

There was optimism for Christians in Sudan when former President Omar Al-Bashir was deposed in a *coup d'état* in April 2019 following months of civil protests and uprisings.[471] President Al-Bashir had run the country under a strict interpretation of *Shari'a* law, which led to persecution of Christians, so when he was removed from office there was a widespread hope that religious freedom would be introduced.[472] The initial signs were encouraging: the death penalty was no longer applied to incidents of apostasy thanks to a series of wide-ranging amendments to criminal law made in July 2020.[473] Public flogging was also ended and the consumption of alcohol by non-Muslims was permitted.[474] In a televised interview, the then Sudanese Justice Minister Nasredeen Abdulbari said: "All these changes are aiming at achieving equality in front of the laws. We have dropped all the articles that had led to any kind of discrimination."[475]

But the prejudice against Christians and other religious minorities, deeply engrained in Sudanese society, was not going to be overturned quickly. For example, between 18th December 2019 and 29th January 2020, one Sudanese Church of Christ (SCOC) church in Jabarona, near Khartoum, was attacked four times. Church leaders said they received threats from Islamist extremists, with one threat stating: "If the government gives you permission to build a church here, they'd better be prepared to collect your dead bodies."[476]

With another military coup in October 2021, Christians were fearful and anxious. The Prime Minister, Abdalla Hamdok, was temporarily detained, along with many other members of the civilian government.[477] Sudan's top general, Abdel Fattah Al-Burhan, took over. The aftermath of this coup has seen individuals connected to the ruling party of former President Al-Bashir re-appointed to official roles, and the undermining of transitional institutions that attempt to hold the former regime to account.[478] Speaking to Open Doors following the coup, a source inside the country said: "We ask you just to pray for Sudan. Pray for the coming hours. We hope that some changes will happen in a peaceful way, we hope that." Open Doors placed Sudan at number 13 on their World Watch List.[479]

Bishop Yunan Tombe Trille, president of the Sudan Catholic Bishops' Conference said: "The international community should put their pressure on the junta to value the life of their citizens and to hand back the power to civil government."[480]

Since the coup, there have been a number of incidents of persecution, both in Sudan and neighbouring South Sudan. In May 2021, an attack on the village of Dungob Alei, in the north of South Sudan, resulted in the death of 13 people and left eight injured.[481] In a statement, the Episcopal Church of South Sudan said that its Diocese of Abyei sits in the most northerly part of South Sudan, in "an area that experiences Islamic encroachments followed by harassment, intimidation and frequent attacks carried out by Arab Islamic militias".[482] Michael Deng Bol, Anglican Bishop of Abyei, said the village "had been barbarically attacked by militiamen of Sudan".[483]

January 2021 A church in Tamboul, Gezira state belonging to the Sudanese Church of Christ (SCOC), was torched on Sunday 3rd. It was reported that a boy aged 13 set fire to the church with petrol after being told to do so by an adult. Police filed a case against the boy on Wednesday 6th but did not charge the adult who allegedly supplied the petrol.[484]

July 2021 Boutros Badawi, an advisor to Sudan's Minister of Religious Affairs and a Christian activist, was attacked in the capital Khartoum. According to CSW, he was attacked on the evening of 2nd July by armed men who beat and threatened him: "One assailant pointed a gun at Mr Badawi's head and threatened to kill him if he continued to say anything about confiscated properties belonging to churches, or the issues surrounding the Sudan Presbyterian Evangelical Church committees."[485]

February 2022 According to SCOC sources in the country, Christian leaders were detained and questioned after Islamist extremists, angry at their presence, locked their building shut. The extremists locked the building of the SCOC in Al Hag Abdalla, roughly 85 miles south-east of Khartoum in Madani, Gezira state, on 21st February. Dalman Hassan, an evangelist for SCOC, who was arrested and released on 27th February, said the extremists accused the Christians of hostility toward Islam by holding gatherings on Friday, the Islamic day of prayer. The church was also accused of providing food to children to try and convert them to Christianity, and stealing the land for their worship building.[486]

April 2022 A pastor was sentenced to a month in prison under a law against disturbing the peace, after being attacked during a worship service. Muslim judge Awad Ibrahim Kury found Pastor Stephanou Adil Kujo and elder Ibrahim Kodi guilty of disturbing the peace under Article 69 of Sudan's 1991 penal code. As a result, the pair were sentenced to one month in prison, beginning on Monday 25th, according to the Christians' attorney, Shanabo Awad.[487] Islamist extremists disrupted worship and attacked three Christians during an SCOC service in Al Hag Abdalla, on 10th April. Pastor Kajo was punched and had his shirt torn, while two women of the congregation were also assaulted, the judge said. Bibles were torn up and chairs were broken by the attackers.

May 2022 A couple were charged with "adultery" because a *Shari'a* court annulled their marriage on the grounds of the husband's conversion to Christianity. They could now face up to 100 lashes. Hamouda Tia Kafi, 34, and Nada Hamad Shukralah, 25, of Al Bageir, Gezira state, were Muslim when they married in 2016 but in 2018 Mr Kafi converted to Christianity. His wife's family sought and won a *Shari'a* court decision to dissolve the marriage on the basis of apostasy, which at the time was punishable by death. However, in 2020 after the end of Omar Al-Bashir's Islamist regime, apostasy was decriminalised. In 2021, Shukralah also converted to Christianity and returned to her husband with their two children. Subsequently, her brother charged the couple with adultery under Article 146 of Sudan's 1991 criminal law.[488]

May 2022 A court approved the demolition of a *c.* 2,400-yard^2 (2,000 m^2) block of properties belonging to the Sudan Presbyterian Evangelical Church in the country's second city, Omdurman.[489]

September 2022 Four Christian converts facing the death penalty for apostasy had all charges dismissed by the court on Thursday 8th. Badar Haroun Abdul-Jabbar, Mohamed Haroun Abdul-Jabbar, Tariq Ared Abdallah and Mortada Ismael Yousef were detained for questioning on 24th June in Zalingei. Five days later they were arrested and sent to the main prison in Zalingei, Central Darfur, before being granted bail on 6th July. The prosecutor told them they would face the death penalty for refusing to renounce their Christian faith, and not agreeing to refrain from praying, evangelising, or participating in Christian activities.[490]

Fears for the long-term future of Christianity in Syria grew over the period under review. An exodus sparked by genocidal violence and extreme poverty gave rise to reports that, after a decade of civil war, the Christian population had "dramatically" declined.[491] Returning from the capital, Damascus, in March 2022, Regina Lynch, International Director of Projects for Aid to the Church in Need (ACN), stated that "despair is common among Syrian Christians".[492] Syriac Catholic Patriarch Ignatius Joseph III Younan of Antioch warned ACN of a continuing exodus, saying "[W]e are very, very scared that it will be the end of Christians… in a few years" not just in Syria but across "the whole of the Middle East".[493] Others, however, said some wanted to stay, and looked to the Church for hope.[494]

Syria's Christian population fell from 1.5 million before the conflict began in 2011 to perhaps 450,000 in 2019.[495] In August 2021, Christian political leaders reported that within a decade, numbers had declined

significantly from 10 percent of the population to a fraction of that figure.[496] For example, over that period Christians in the Kurdish Jazira region in the north-east had decreased from 150,000 to 55,000.[497] Church and public sources lead ACN to suggest that today Christians in Syria number between 200,000 and 400,000.

A primary driver of Christian emigration is the desire "to escape"[498] mandatory military service, which carries a high risk of injury or death, and can last a decade. As a result of mass migration of men, some Christians communities have a major gender ratio imbalance among young people. In the Valley of the Christians, near Homs, 60-70 percent of young people are women, according to the local Church.

In many parts of the country, Christians were "driven out" en masse by genocidal violence, as highlighted in media coverage at the time.[499] The rise of Daesh (ISIS), and the systematic persecution of Christians and other minorities, had forced entire towns and villages into exile abroad, the vast majority of whom never return.[500] In much of the country, the problem of militant extremism has much improved, with forces loyal to Syria's President Bashar Al-Assad re-taking towns and cities captured by militant Islamist groups, such as Daesh or Tahrir Al-Sham. In government-controlled areas, the Church can freely conduct its liturgies and internal governance, as well as some social and charitable activities, but, like other religious groups, it is strictly monitored and lacks the freedom to comment on public affairs.

Although the Daesh threat subsided, nevertheless Christians "reportedly continued to face discrimination and violence at the hands of violent extremist groups."[501] Daesh was reportedly responsible for 640 attacks in Syria from October 2019-June 2020.[502] There were frequent reports of the Islamist militants targeting Christian-majority towns and villages in Idlib governorate in the north-west.

A number of Islamist extremist groups subjugated Christians, forcing them to live under strict *Shari'a* Islamic law, including mandatory *jizya* tax. The Al-Qaeda offshoot Hay'at Tahrir Al-Sham (HTS) was accused of seeking to "brutalise minority communities".[503] In villages north of Jisr Al-Shughur, HTS reportedly displaced large numbers of Christians, converting some homes into mosques. The 60 Christian families allowed to remain were reportedly only permitted to pray within churches, some of which were in ruins and then only on condition that bells were not rung nor crosses placed on public view. By March 2022, Christians from the region reported that in some of their villages up to 95 percent of the faithful had fled[504] – in Idlib, there are now only 210 families left, mostly Greek-Orthodox families, consisting of one or two elderly persons.

Turkish-led or inspired attacks on towns populated by Christians in the extreme north represented a critical threat to the community at large *(see June 2021, September 2021, January 2022)*.[505]

In the country as a whole, Christians, in common with so many others, suffered from the devastating effects of spiralling economic crisis. ACN Syria project partner Sister Annie Demerjian described seeing "children and women looking in bins, desperate for food".[506] According to the World

Health Organisation, up to 90 percent of the people were living below the poverty line[507] with more than 9.3 million people lacking adequate food.[508] Nearly half the pre-war population of Syria had been forced to flee their homes. There were reportedly 6.7 million people displaced within the country[509] and a further 6.6 million now abroad as refugees.[510]

November 2020 Turkish-supported Syrian armed opposition groups attacked the predominantly Christian city of Al-Suqyiabiyah.[511]

June 2021 Three Orthodox Christian men – Jamil Gorges, Amad Jassim Suud and Muhsin Garbhi Ahli – were arrested in a village outside the northern Syrian town of Ras Al-Ain. They were taken across the border by the Turkish forces, found guilty on "thinly evidenced terror charges" and jailed for life by a Turkish court. Lawyers said the verdict "violates Turkish and international humanitarian law and reflects the unlawful action of Turkish forces and their Sunni rebel proxies in the large swathes of territory that Turkey occupies in northern Syria."[512]

September 2021 Christian leaders in north-east Syria accused Turkey of carrying out targeted attacks against the Christian majority town of Tel-Tamer and surrounding villages. Bassam Ishak, president of Christian political group the Syriac National Council, said the Turkish bombing had caused a mass exodus of Christians.[513] The UN commission of Inquiry on Syria has accused Turkish-backed Syrian groups of committing war crimes against minorities in northern Syria. Human Rights organisations have accused these groups of forcing demographic change by pushing out indigenous residents.[514]

December 2021 Chaldean Catholic priest Father Nidal Abdel Massih Thomas, patriarchal vicar for north-eastern Syria, said that of the 21,000 Syriac Orthodox in the Jazira region in 2011, only 800 remain. He said migration meant only two of the many churches in the 38 villages across the region were still active. He said the exodus began in 2017 when 150 Christians were kidnapped.[515]

January 2022 Melkite Greek Catholic Archbishop Jean Abdo Arbach of Homs told ACN that economic catastrophe meant the situation was in many ways worse than during the war. He said soaring inflation meant

that medical surgery had risen from 200,000 Syrian Lira, on average, before the war, to 2 million. He added economic collapse was prompting many families to flee, including those who had survived bombardment and severe hardship during the war.[516]

January 2022 Mar Sawa Al-Hakim Church in the village of Tel-Tamer, in north-east Syria, was attacked. Houses and other buildings were also damaged. Syriac Orthodox Archbishop Mar Maurice Amseeh of Jazira and Euphrates, said the attacks reflected Turkey's expansionist ambitions which aim to empty the area of Christians.[517]

February 2022 90-year-old Christian man Michel Butros Al-Jisri reflected on the drastic decline of Christians in Idlib city, northern Syria. He described how family members gradually left the city, but he refuses to leave. "My family is from Idlib city. My family and I used to live here in this house, which became a part of me and I shall not leave it, come what may." In Idlib, Christians once numbered 10,000, but an exodus sparked by extremists taking control means that the faithful now make up less than one percent of the city's population.[518]

March 2022 The Syriac Catholic Church held its first nationwide meeting in Damascus, focusing on the Church's charitable work in the country.[519]

March 2022 Returning from a meeting of bishops in Damascus, Regina Lynch, ACN's International Director of Projects said that in a situation where 90 percent live below the poverty line "despair is common among Syria's Christians". But she added that the Church and its commitment to providing emergency support meant that although "many Christians are short of hope, any they do find is in the initiatives of the Church."[520]

June 2022 Closed to the outside world because of civil war and the COVID-19 pandemic, Deir Mar Musa Al Habashi Monastery finally reopened to pilgrims. The ancient monastic site, more than 60 miles north of Damascus, attracted renewed international attention when Jesuit Father Paolo Dall'Oglio, who is still missing after being kidnapped by militant Islamists, turned it into a centre for dialogue between Islam and Christianity. Abbot Jihad Youssef said: "For many Syrians, the abbey represents a spiritual oasis for people from different religious backgrounds."[521]

June 2022 Maronite Archbishop Samir Nassar of Damascus said the "bombs" of poverty and hunger, trauma and displacement have weakened the community. Reporting that church-going had declined, he said that the family is today "dispersed, deprived of resources, without shelter, overwhelmed by pain, devastated by disease". He said the situation was made worse by long-term military service where young people were forced to choose between life on the battle front or dodging conscription.[522]

July 2022 Two were killed and 12 injured during an attack on a Greek Orthodox church being built in Al-Suqaylabiyah, Hama Governorate on Sunday 24th. The Hagia Sophia Church's design was based on the historic church in Istanbul of the same name. The aerial bombardment occurred during the church's inauguration ceremony.[523]

August-September 2022 Delegates who had visited Syria told the eleventh assembly of the World Council of Churches, in Karlsruhe, Germany that it was essential to help the region's Christians stay in their homelands.

TURKEY

The transformation of Istanbul's historic Hagia Sophia into a mosque could be said to symbolise an increasing shift from pluralism to Islamism within the country. Hagia Sophia was a museum when the change was announced, having been built as a Greek Orthodox Basilica in 537AD, and then converted into a mosque following the fall of Constantinople in 1453. President Recep Tayyip Erdoğan supported the development: declaring in March 2019 that the Hagia Sophia would formally become a mosque again, a move confirmed by a July 2020 decision of the Council of Ministers.[524] The Ecumenical Patriarch Bartholomew I said: "The conversion of Hagia Sophia into a mosque will disappoint millions of Christians around the world, and Hagia Sophia, which, due to its sacredness, is a vital centre where East is embraced with the West, will fracture these two worlds".[525]

In August 2020, President Erdoğan also ordered that Chora Museum, famous for its late Medieval Christian frescoes and mosaics, be reconverted into a mosque. Unique in having most of its original artworks still intact, these were covered with white cloths in October so that Islamic worship could resume on the site.[526] Inaugural prayers scheduled for 30th October, due to be attended by President Erdoğan, were cancelled, ostensibly to allow for restoration work, following news that UNESCO was sending delegations (October 2020 and January-

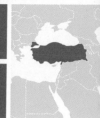
February 2021) to Chora and Hagia Sophia.[527] In July 2021, UNESCO's World Heritage Committee expressed "intense concern" over the changes, which had not been carried out in accordance with the organisation's guidelines.[528]

Speaking to ACN in May 2022, Archbishop Martin Kmetec of Izmir said: "I would not say that Christians are generally being discriminated against. But negative incidents do occur when dealing with authorities and administrative bodies. The Catholic Church is not recognised as a legal entity." The 1923 Lausanne Treaty only grants legal minority status to Armenian Apostolic Orthodox Christians, Greek Orthodox Christians and Jews. Other Christians have no legal identity and cannot corporately own property or seek legal redress – currently they own property through separate foundations. All jobs related to religion (teachers of religion, ministers, etc.) depend on the Diyanet for their appointments, training and salaries. The Diyanet is the state religious affairs directorate which oversees all religious matters, a mandate which frequently extends to Christian communities even though constitutionally its role is "to execute the works concerning the beliefs, worship, and ethics of *Islam*, enlighten the public about their religion, and administer the sacred worshipping places" (Italics mine). Christian Churches continue to face restrictions on the training of their clergy, and the Greek Orthodox Church's Halki Seminary remains closed 50 years after it was shut *(see December 2021 below)*.[529]

The village of Mehr in the south-east illustrates the ongoing problems faced by Turkey's different Christian communities. It was a Chaldean majority village before fighting between the PKK (the Kurdistan Workers Party) and the Turkish army led to it being evacuated in 1989 and 1992. Around 2011 a small number of Chaldeans returned to the village to rebuild the Christian presence there. Married couple Hormoz and Simoni Diril were the first to return – and at the time their son Fr Adday Ramzi Diril was the only priest ministering to *c.* 7,000 Iraqi Christian refugees living in Turkey (in April 2022 a second priest was ordained). In January 2020 the

couple went missing, Simoni Diril was later found dead. In May 2021 the village's historic cave church was vandalised and desecrated *(see below)*.[530]

There are more than 4 million refugees and asylum-seekers in Turkey, among them thousands of Arabic-speaking Catholics, mostly from the Chaldean and Syriac Churches. Based in more than 80 cities, they cannot leave the town where they first register. Speaking in June 2022 Bishop Paolo Bizzeti, Vicar Apostolic of Anatolia, warned that these Christian refugees "do not have meeting places, buildings for worship, cannot move freely or participate in celebrations." Arabic-speaking priests travel from city to city to minister to them.[531]

February 2021 Concerns were raised over the expulsions of almost 70 Christian foreign nationals since early 2019 as part of what was described by CSW as "an ongoing campaign targeting Protestant denominations". Those expelled included individuals married to Turkish citizens. Most of those affected took part in Church training seminars in late 2019 and early 2020.[532]

March 2021 Fears were expressed that a monastery with historical monument status could collapse if a multi-storey car park was built on land seized by authorities in 1969. The Syriac Catholic Foundation, which owns St Efram's Syriac Catholic Monastery where there has been no community since 1933, tweeted on Thursday 1st: "The Municipality, which years ago expropriated a part of the land owned by the historical St Efram Syriac Catholic Monastery in Mardin, as being 'green space' is now building a multilevel car park on top, knowing that the foundations of the historical building will be damaged and destroyed in that area."[533]

April 2021 Father Sefer Aho Bileçen of St Yacoub's Syriac Orthodox Monastery in Nusaybin was sentenced to two years and one month in jail for "supporting a terrorist organisation", after giving bread and water to individuals who came to his monastery. The Turkish government claims they were known members of the PKK. Throughout his trial in a closed courtroom Father Aho maintained that he was unaware of the individuals' political affiliation and said he would have helped anyone who asked.[534]

May 2021 Marta Shimoni Church in Mehr was desecrated on Tuesday 11th. Crosses, icons, and other church items were found strewn across the path leading to the cave church's entrance."[535]

August 2021 Headstones were removed and the bones from graves scattered in a Christian cemetery in Tuşba District, Van Province. Local sources suggested a landowner caused the damage, bringing bulldozers into the Armenian Christian graveyard.[536]

December 2021 This month marked half a century since the Greek-Orthodox Halki Seminary, located on Heybeliada island, south of Istanbul, was closed. The seminary was founded in 1844, repurposing part of the monastery of the Holy Trinity, originally founded by Patriarch St Photius I in the ninth century. In 1971, the government nationalised all higher-education institutions, forcing the seminary to shut as it would not accept state control.[537]

March 2022 On Thursday 31st the Diyanet announced that Tarawih prayers, evening devotions for Ramadan, would be said in the Hagia Sophia for the first time in 88 years. The prayers were scheduled on Fridays, Saturdays and Sundays with immediate effect. Previously COVID-19 restrictions had prevented public prayers taking place there.[538]

April 2022 The trial began of three men accused of kidnapping the elderly parents of a Chaldean Catholic priest in January 2020. Simoni Diril was later found dead, while her husband Hormoz is still missing.

August-September 2022 St Efram's Syriac Orthodox Church was set to open. It is the first completely new church built since the foundation of the Republic of Turkey in 1922. [539]

VIETNAM

There is an ongoing problem with legislation being used to restrict religious practice. As the United States Commission on International Religious Freedom (USCIRF) noted:

> Government authorities have continued to use the 2018 Law on Belief and Religion – including complex registration requirements and vaguely worded national security provisions – to actively restrict religious freedom in Vietnam. The law, as written and implemented, contravenes international human rights standards and systematically violates religious freedom, particularly of independent religious groups.

While the commission found "some notable improvements" in the legislation, for example it reduced the waiting period religious organisations had to observe before they could register with the government, nevertheless USCIRF found that "the 2018 Law imposes burdensome and complex requirements on religious groups to register with the government". One example of these improvements would be the Catholic parish in Sơn La Province being formally approved after waiting several years *(see November 2021 below)*. USCIRF noted that separate registration processes were required for various religious activities and gatherings, as well as official recognition.[540] Based on the issues it observed in 2021, USCIRF recommended that Vietnam be designated as a Country of Particular Concern.[541] In June 2022 the Government Committee for Religious Affairs (GCRA) released two draft decrees on religion for consultation, which would supersede the 2018 Law on Belief and Religion, and sanction new penalties for violations.

POPULATION
98 million

CHRISTIAN POPULATION
9 million

RELIGIONS
Buddhists 50.25% Traditional 21.25%
Atheists 12% Christians 9% Others 7.5%

Christians belonging to the H'Mong and Montagnard ethnic groups in Vietnam's highlands continue to be singled out for harassment, such as the Ha Mon religious community, a radical Montagnard Catholic group, and the Montagnard Evangelical Church of Christ. More than other groups they have had services disrupted and endured other forms of harassment, with unregistered groups suffering particularly egregiously.[542] The Montagnard Evangelical Church of Christ saw their Christmas activities disrupted by police in Sông Hinh District in 2021 *(see below)*.

A particular problem that churches have faced over the years has been the requisitioning of property. This may be more related to the desire to acquire prime parcels of land, rather than a particular animus against religion, but highlights that the rights of religious groups are not widely respected. In 2021, An Hòa parish petitioned local authorities to stop construction of new houses on the land next door to their parish. The parish insists that it owns the land, previously the site of a Catholic school, but in 1975 agreed that the state could develop space for local artisans, and allotments for parishioners there. These never materialised and in 2019 the parish formally requested that the land be returned. The then Prime Minister Nguyễn Tấn Dũng issued a directive on religious groups' property in 2008, saying state bodies could continue using land so long as it was done appropriately and effectively, otherwise, the land would be returned to the religious group or another body would be given administrative control. However, some authorities have continued to let third-parties exploit property owned by religious groups.[543]

Nonetheless, the scope for Christian groups to carry out activities seems to be widening in some areas. During the COVID-19 pandemic, local Churches responded to authorities' invitations to help caring for hospital patients.[544] Parishes were unhampered as they undertook charitable activities, including food distributions.[545] In December 2021, Hồ Chí Minh City Communist Party returned five properties to the Catholic Church in thanks for its work tackling coronavirus.[546]

November 2020 The Evangelical Church of Vietnam's 10th Congress of the Clergy Council was cancelled by the Government Committee for Religious Affairs.[547]

January 2021 Five members of the Montagnard Evangelical Church of Christ were forced to renounce their faith publicly on Friday 15th. Police from Ea Lâm village, Phú Yên Province, brought the Christians to Pung tribal village where they were told to recant their belief in front of 20 witnesses. They were threatened with jail and even death if they did not recant.[548]

May 2021 Revival Ekklesia Mission, based in Hồ Chí Minh City, had its registration "temporarily suspended" after Church members contracted COVID-19. Vietnam's track and trace system allegedly identified 211 cases connected with them after two members went to Gia Định General Hospital with serious coronavirus symptoms. On Sunday 30th, the deputy minister of Home Affairs, and chairman of the Government Committee for Religious Affairs, General Vũ Chiến Thắng, threatened Revival Ekklesia Mission with penalties including "permanent erasure" if serious violations were found to have occurred. According to the Mission's leader Rev'd Võ Xuân Loan, the church had largely gone online, even before authorities stopped gatherings of more than 20 people. Authorities tested those working at the Mission's two Hà Nội branches but obtained negative results.[549]

July 2021 USCIRF condemned a raid by authorities on two churches in Đắk Lắk Province, leading to the detention of up to two dozen Christians from the Montagnard ethnic group.[550]

November 2021 A Catholic parish in Sơn La province was officially recognised by authorities, after having existed underground for 30 years. Mộc Châu Parish, which was formally established in 2015, is the first parish in Sơn La to be formally approved. There are seven other parishes in Sơn La which are not recognised.[551]

December 2021 The funeral of H'Mong Christian leader Dương Văn Minh on Sunday 12th was disrupted by c. 300 police officers in riot gear accompanied by individuals wearing medical hazard suits. Authorities claimed they were implementing COVID-19 safety. One Christian reported authorities set up checkpoints around the villages where members of Pastor Văn Minh's movement lived on the grounds of preventing the virus' spread: "When we asked whether there were COVID-19 virus infections in the area, some mobile police officers said no, adding that they had just been asked to block the area." 36 people were arrested.[552]

December 2021 On Christmas Eve, police in Ea Lâm Commune, Phú Yên Province entered the home of Pastor Y Cuốn Niê of the Montagnard Evangelical Church of Christ around 10pm to demand he stop the Christmas service he was holding. The pastor was taken to Sông Hinh police station for questioning. Pastor Niê said that his congregation had sought to meet the registration requirements under the 2018 Law on Belief and Religion.[553]

January 2022 A Bible study in a private home in Huế Province was broken up by police who confiscated all the Christian materials on Sunday 30th. Homeowner Lê Thị Hoa, who lives in A Ngô Commune, A Lưới District, was accused of illegally holding a religious gathering, after a neighbour informed on them. Authorities said the meetings must stop as it was a "Communist village".[554]

February 2022 Government officials disrupted Mass in Vu Bản, Hòa Bình Province on Sunday 20th. Officials shouted at Archbishop Giuse (Joseph) Vũ Văn Thiên of Hà Nội to stop immediately and dismiss worshippers. The Catholics managed to eject officials and resume Mass. Fr Nguyễn Văn Khải said: "This is the first time I've ever seen local government officials approach the altar to disrupt the Holy Mass without even waiting for it to end before harassing priests as they used to do in the past".[555]

May 2022 15 Christians arrested at the funeral of Pastor Dương Văn Minh *(see December 2021 above)* received jail sentences of up to four years in two closed trials held in late May. They were found guilty of "resisting officers on duty" and "violating regulations on safety in crowded areas".[556]

July 2022 Reports suggested authorities in Nghệ An Province are trying to create "Christian-free Zones", pressuring animists to drive out Christians. In Kỳ Sơn District, police have threatened H'Mong Christian converts, demanding they return to animism.[557]

Endnotes

1 John Newton, "Islamist captors beat nun for praying", *ACN (UK) News*, 18th January 2022, https://acnuk.org/news/mali-islamist-captors-beat-nun-for-praying/ [accessed 26/07/22].
2 Ibid.
3 "Harassment of religious groups reaches new peak in 2019", *Pew Research Center*, 30th September 2021, https://www.pewresearch.org/religion/2021/09/30/harassment-of-religious-groups-reaches-new-peak-in-2019/ [accessed 26/07/22].
4 Ibid.
5 David Curry, president of Open Doors (USA), quoted in Jayson Casper, "The 50 Countries where it's Hardest to Follow Jesus in 2022", *Christianity Today*, 19th January 2022 https://www.christianitytoday.com/news/2022/january/christian-persecution-2022-countries-killed-world-list.html [accessed 26/07/22].
6 Ibid.
7 Egypt is not included as it is categorised as part of the Middle East.
8 Jared Thompson, "Examining Extremism: Islamic State in the Greater Sahara", *Center for Strategic & International Studies*, July 22nd 2021, https://www.csis.org/blogs/examining-extremism/examining-extremism-islamic-state-greater-sahara [accessed 11/07/22]
9 Ibid.
10 Fionn Shiner, "Fear and panic as Daesh 'seize' town", *ACN (UK) News*, March 30th 2021, https://acnuk.org/news/mozambique-fear-and-panic-as-daesh-seize-town/ [accessed 11/04/22].
11 See "Nigeria" country entry in *Persecuted and Forgotten?* 2020-2022.
12 Wale Odunsi, "Religious intolerance: 'Boko Haram, ISWAP, bandits killing Christians' – CAN chides US govt", *[Nigeria] Daily Post*, 21st November 2021 https://dailypost.ng/2021/11/21/religious-intolerance-boko-haram-iswap-bandits-killing-christians-can-chides-us-govt/ [accessed 25/05/22].
13 Charles Collins, "UK Foreign Office asked to help religious minorities during coronavirus pandemic", *Crux*, 3rd June 2020, https://cruxnow.com/church-in-uk-and-ireland/2020/06/uk-foreign-office-asked-to-help-religious-minorities-during-coronavirus-pandemic [accessed 29/07/22].
14 "Four men charged with apostasy", *CSW*, July 8th 2022, https://www.csw.org.uk/2022/07/08/press/5766/article.htm [accessed 12/07/22].
15 Duarte Mendonca, "Ethiopian Orthodox Church Patriarch condemns Tigray 'genocide'", *CNN*, 8th May 2021, https://edition.cnn.com/2021/05/08/africa/orthodox-church-tigray-ethiopia-intl/index.html [accessed 30/05/22].
16 Fionn Shiner, "'Genocide is happening in Tigray'", *ACN (UK) News*, 28th May 2021, https://acnuk.org/news/ethiopia-genocide-is-happening-in-tigray/ [accessed 30/05/22].
17 The Pew figures released in September 2021 analyse the condition in China relating to 2019, while this falls just outside of the period examined by this report it is indicative of the scale of problems faced by Christians and other religious groups in China. *Globally, Social Hostilities Related to Religion Decline in 2019, While Government Restrictions Remain at Highest Levels* (Pew Research Centre, 2021 report), p. 61 https://www.pewresearch.org/religion/wp-content/uploads/sites/7/2021/09/PF_09.30.21_religious.restrictions_AppendixA.pdf [accessed 14/07/22].
18 John Pontifex, "Pakistan Christians denied food aid", *ACN (UK) News*, 2nd April 2020 https://acnuk.org/news/pakistan-christians-denied-food-aid/ [accessed 11/07/22].

19 John Pontifex, "Christians denied COVID-19 food aid", *ACN (UK) News*, 12th May 2020 https://acnuk.org/news/pakistan-christians-denied-covid-19-aid/ [accessed 11/07/22].
20 See Marwan Abu-Ghazaleh Mahajneh, Itay Greenspan and Muhammad M. Haj-Yahia, "Zakat giving to Non-Muslims: Muftis' attitudes in Arab and Non-Arab countries", *Journal of Muslim Philanthropy and Civil Society* 5.2, pp.66-86.
21 Fionn Shiner, "'Christian persecution never ended in Middle East'", *ACN (UK) News*, 6th July 2022 https://acnuk.org/news/united-kingdom-middle-east-christian-persecution-never-ended-in-middle-east/ [accessed 27/07/22].
22 "Afghanistan", *World Watch List 2022* https://media.opendoorsuk.org/document/pdf/2022-Dossiers/Advocacy-Dossier-Afghanistan.pdf [accessed 27/05/22].
23 Kamran Chaudhry, "Afghan Christians find new hope in Pakistan", *UCA News*, 23rd June 2022 https://www.ucanews.com/news/afghan-christians-find-new-hope-in-pakistan/97758 [accessed 20/07/22].
24 US State Dept., "Afghanistan", *2021 Report on International Religious Freedom* https://www.state.gov/reports/2021-report-on-international-religious-freedom/afghanistan/ [accessed 17/06/22].
25 Ibid.
26 Ibid.
27 Ibid.
28 Ibid.
29 USCIRF, "Afghanistan", *2022 Annual Report* https://www.uscirf.gov/sites/default/files/2022-04/2022%20USCIRF%20Annual%20Report_1.pdf [accessed 27/05/2]
30 Kelsey Zorzi, "Afghanistan's Christians are turning off phones and going into hiding", *The Hill*, 23rd August 2021 https://thehill.com/opinion/international/568992-afghanistans-christians-are-turning-off-phones-and-going-into-hiding [accessed 27/05/22]; "Afghanistan", *World Watch List 2022*, op. cit.
31 Niala Mohammad, "Factsheet: Afghanistan", *USCIRF*, October 2021 https://www.uscirf.gov/sites/default/files/2021-10/2021%20Factsheet%20-%20Religious%20Minorities%20in%20Afghanistan.pdf [accessed 27/05/22].
32 "Afghanistan", *World Watch List 2022*, op. cit.
33 Ibid.
34 US State Dept., "Afghanistan", *2021*, op. cit.
35 Ibid.
36 Ibid.
37 Ibid.
38 USCIRF, "Afghanistan", *2022*, op. cit.
39 Ibid.
40 Christine Rousselle and Jose Torres, Jr., "Terrified Christians in Afghanistan brace for attack: 'We are coming for you'", *Catholic News Agency*, 19th August 2021 https://www.catholicnewsagency.com/news/248726/terrified-christians-in-afghanistan-brace-for-attacks-we-are-coming-for-you [accessed 26/05/22].
41 RNS Press Release Distribution Service, "Media ministry offers 'lifeline' to fearful Afghans as Taliban kill Christians", *Religion News Service*, 17th August 2021 https://religionnews.com/2021/08/17/media-ministry-offers-lifeline-to-fearful-afghans-as-taliban-kill-christians/ [accessed 26/05/22].
42 "Taliban Forbids People from Evacuating Afghanistan", *International Christian Concern*, 2nd March 2022 https://www.persecution.org/2022/03/02/taliban-forbids-people-evacuating-afghanistan/ [accessed 26/05/22].
43 Katey Hearth, "Death surrounds believers in Afghanistan", *Mission Network News*, 3rd April 2022 https://chvnradio.com/articles/death-surrounds-believers-in-afghanistan [accessed 26/05/22].

44 Claire Evans, "Escape or Stay in Afghanistan?", *International Christian Concern,* 21st April 2022 https://www.persecution.org/2022/04/21/escape-stay-afghanistan/ [accessed 26/05/22].

45 "More than 1,000 civilians have died in Myanmar unrest, say activists", *Guardian,* 9th August 2021 https://www.theguardian.com/world/2021/aug/19/more-than-1000-civilians-have-died-in-myanmar-unrest-say-activists [accessed 06/05/22].

46 John Newton, "The killings must stop at once", *ACN (UK) News,* 15th March 2021 https://acnuk.org/news/myanmar-the-killings-must-stop-at-once/ [accessed 06/06/22].

47 All figures in this paragraph taken from "At least 132 religious buildings destroyed since Myanmar coup", *Radio Free Asia,* 8th July 2022 https://www.rfa.org/english/news/myanmar/religiousbuildings-07082022181759.html [accessed 21/07/22].

48 "A Catholic church hit by rockets, Baptist churches burned down", *Fides,* 10th November http://www.fides.org/en/news/71112-ASIA_MYANMAR_A_Catholic_church_hit_by_rockets_Baptist_churches_burned_down ; "Attacks on churches, the Bishop of Pekhon: it means "attacking the hearts of each of the faithful", *Fides,* 1st December 2021 http://www.fides.org/en/news/71230-ASIA_MYANMAR_Attacks_on_churches_the_Bishop_of_Pekhon_it_means_attacking_the_hearts_of_each_of_the_faithful both sites [accessed 23/03/22].

49 "Over 100 Religious Buildings Destroyed by Myanmar Regime Forces", *Irrawaddy,* 28th March 2022 https://www.irrawaddy.com/news/burma/over-100-religious-buildings-destroyed-by-myanmar-regime-forces.html [accessed 31/03/22].

50 John Pontifex and John Newton, *Persecuted and Forgotten? 2011-2013,* p. 28.

51 US State Dept., "Burma", *2020 Report on International Religious Freedom,* https://www.state.gov/reports/2020-report-on-international-religious-freedom/burma/ [accessed 24/03/22].

52 Ibid.

53 "Catholic priest arrested by the military has been released", *Fides,* 18th May http://www.fides.org/en/news/70141-ASIA_MYANMAR_Catholic_priest_arrested_by_the_military_has_been_released [accessed 22/03/22].

54 "Two young people killed in the compound of the Catholic Cathedral surrounded by the military", *Fides,* 8th March 2022 http://www.fides.org/en/news/69741-ASIA_MYANMAR_Two_young_people_killed_in_the_compound_of_the_Catholic_Cathedral_surrounded_by_the_military ; "'Shoot me instead': Myanmar nun's plea to spare protesters", *Guardian,* 9th March 2021 https://www.theguardian.com/world/2021/mar/09/shoot-me-instead-myanmar-nuns-plea-to-spare-protesters both sites [accessed 21/07/22].

55 John Newton, "Cardinal condemns shelling of church", *ACN (UK) News,* 27th May 2021 https://acnuk.org/news/burma-cardinal-condemns-shelling-of-church/ [accessed 23/03/22].

56 "Three Pastors of the Baptist Church arrested in Kachin State: they were praying for peace", *Fides,* 1st July 2021 http://www.fides.org/en/news/70421-ASIA_MYANAMR_Three_Pastors_of_the_Baptist_Church_arrested_in_Kachin_State_they_were_praying_for_peace [accessed 23/03/22].

57 "After arrest by local militia in Chin State: priest and catechist return to pastoral service", *Fides,* 23rd August 2021 http://www.fides.org/en/news/70677-ASIA_MYANMAR_After_arrest_by_local_militia_in_Chin_State_priest_and_catechist_return_to_pastoral_service [accessed 22/03/22].

58 "Burmese army soldiers occupy and desecrate two churches", *Fides,* 1st September 2021 http://www.fides.org/en/news/70717-ASIA_MYANMAR_Burmese_army_soldiers_occupy_and_desecrate_two_churches [accessed 23/03/22].

59 The pastor's name is also gives in several sources as "Cung Biah Hum". "Violence of the Burmese army against

civilians: Baptist pastor killed", *Fides,* 22nd September 2021 http://www.fides.org/en/news/70842-ASIA_MYANMAR_Violence_of_the_Burmese_army_against_civilians_Baptist_pastor_killed ; "Thousands flee fighting in Chin state to India", *Asianews,* 23rd September https://www.Asianews.it/news-en/Thousands-flee-fighting-in-Chin-state-to-India-54121.html both sites [accessed 23/03/22].

60 "The funeral of Catholic civilians massacred in Kayah", *Fides,* 29th December http://www.fides.org/en/news/71383-ASIA_MYANMAR_The_funeral_of_Catholic_civilians_massacred_in_Kayah [accessed 22/03/22].

61 "Two Catholic priests arrested for providing humanitarian aid to displaced people", *Fides,* 25th February 2022 http://www.fides.org/en/news/71712-ASIA_MYANMAR_Two_Catholic_priests_arrested_for_providing_humanitarian_aid_to_displaced_people [accessed 22/03/22].

62 "Church and convent bombed in Demoso", *Asianews,* 10th March 2022 https://www.Asianews.it/news-en/Church-and-convent-bombed-in-Demoso-55324.html [accessed 23/03/22].

63 "Archbishop of Mandalay among those detained by military in Cathedral raid", *CSW,* 11th April 2022.

64 "Myanmar Church calls for end to attacks on places of worship", *UCA News,* 9th June 2022 https://www.UCA News.com/news/myanmar-church-calls-for-end-to-attacks-on-places-of-worship/92802 [accessed 21/07/22].

65 US State Dept., "China (Includes Tibet, Xinjiang, Hong Kong, and Macau)", *2020 Report on International Religious Freedom* https://www.state.gov/reports/2020-report-on-international-religious-freedom/china/ [accessed 23/05/22].

66 Ibid.

67 Ibid.

68 Ibid.

69 "Church surveillance, COVID-19 controls affect China's Christians – 1 of 5 global trends", *World Watch Monitor,* 13th January 2022 https://www.worldwatchmonitor.org/2021/01/church-surveillance-covid-19-controls-affect-chinas-christians-1-of-5-global-trends/ [accessed 12/08/22].

70 US State Dept., "China", *2020,* op. cit.

71 Ibid.

72 "Holy See and China renew Provisional Agreement for 2 years", *Vatican News,* 22nd October 2020 https://www.vaticannews.va/en/vatican-city/news/2020-10/holy-see-china-provisional-agreement-renew-appointment-bishops.html [accessed 24/05/22].

73 "Diocese of Xuanhua: In Zhangjiakou, illegitimate priestly ordinations for a 'diocese' that does not exist for the Holy See", *Asianews,* 14th May 2021 https://www.Asianews.it/news-en/Diocese-of-Xuanhua:-In-Zhangjiakou,-illegitimate-priestly-ordinations-for-a-%27diocese%27-that-does-not-exist-for-the-Holy-See-53140.html [accessed 18/05/22].

74 James Roberts, "Mixed church reactions to arrest of Cardinal Zen", *Tablet,* 17th May 2022 https://www.thetablet.co.uk/news/15449/mixed-church-reactions-to-arrest-of-cardinal- [accessed 18/05/22].

75 "Catholic Diocese of Hong Kong faces shortage of Chinese bible due to unwillingness of mainland Chinese printing houses", *ChinaAid,* 1st August 2022 https://www.chinaaid.org/2022/08/catholic-diocese-of-hong-kong-faces.html [accessed 12/05/22].

76 Greg Torode, "Vatican envoy in Hong Kong warns Catholic missions to prepare for China crackdown", *Reuters,* 5th July 2022 https://www.reuters.com/world/asia-pacific/vatican-envoy-hong-kong-warns-catholic-missions-prepare-china-crackdown-2022-07-05/ [accessed 25/07/22].

77 "Chinese Communist Party "secretly" bans all Christmas events but two...", *ChinaAid,* 25th December 2020 https://www.chinaaid.org/2020/12/chinese-communist-party-secretly-bans.html?utm_source=feedburner&utm_medium=email&utm_campaign=Feed%3A+ChinaAid+%28China+Aid%29 [accessed 19/05/22].

78 Wang Zhicheng, "Yining's Sacred Heart church to be torn down", *Asianews,* 19th February 2022 https://www.Asianews.it/news-en/Yining%E2%80%99s-Sacred-Heart-church-to-be-torn-down-52395.html [accessed 20/05/22].

79 "Diocese of Xuanhua: In Zhangjiakou, illegitimate priestly ordinations for a 'diocese' that does not exist for the Holy See", *Asianews,* op. cit.

80 Wang Zhicheng, "Bishop Augustine Cui Tai of Xuanhua is again sequestered by police", *Asianews,* 23rd June 2020 https://www.Asianews.it/news-en/Bishop-Augustine-Cui-Tai-of-Xuanhua-is-again-sequestered-by-police-50421.html [accessed 12/08/22].

81 John Burger, "Chinese authorities arrest bishop, priests, seminarians", *Aleteia,* 26th May 2021 https://aleteia.org/2021/05/26/chinese-authorities-arrest-bishop-priests-seminarians/ ; Wu Xiunying, "Catholic Bishop and 10 Priests detained in Henan", *Bitter Winter,* 22nd July 2021 https://bitterwinter.org/catholic-bishop-and-10-priests-detained-in-henan/ ; "China arrests Vatican-approved bishop, priests, seminarians", *UCA News,* 24th May 2021 https://www.UCA News.com/news/china-arrests-vatican-approved-bishop-priests-seminarians/92587 [accessed 18/07/22].

82 Xiunying, "Catholic Bishop and 10 Priests detained in Henan", *Bitter Winter,* op. cit.

83 Wu Xiunying, "Catholic Bishop Joseph Zhang Weizhu: Still Detained Despite Reported Vatican Intervention", *Bitter Winter,* 5th May 2022 https://bitterwinter.org/bishop-joseph-zhang-weizhu-still-detained/ [accessed 18/05/22]; Michael Haynes, "Underground Chinese bishop still missing after 'illegal' 9-month imprisonment", *LifeSite News,* 23rd February 2022 https://www.lifesitenews.com/news/underground-chinese-bishop-still-missing-after-illegal-9-months-imprisonment/ [accessed 19/05/22].

84 "Christians face arrests, jail terms for church meetings and printing religious texts", *CSW,* 24th November 2021 https://www.csw.org.uk/2021/11/24/press/5489/article.htm [accessed 20/05/22].

85 "Elder of Early Rain Covenant Church arrested on Christmas Eve", *ChinaAid,* 29th December 2021 https://www.chinaaid.org/2021/12/elder-of-early-rain-covenant-church.html [accessed 12/08/22].

86 "House church leader sentenced to eight years in prison on fraud charges", *CSW,* 23rd February 2022 https://www.csw.org.uk/2022/02/23/press/5587/article.htm [accessed 20/05/22].

87 "Indictment papers for Hubei Christians released", *ChinaAid,* 17th January 2020 https://www.chinaaid.org/2020/01/indictment-papers-for-hubei-christians.html [accessed 20/05/22].

88 James Roberts, "Mixed church reactions to arrest of Cardinal Zen", op. cit.

89 Tiffany Wertheimer, "Hong Kong cardinal Joseph Zen arrested under China's security law", *BBC News,* 12th May 2022 https://www.bbc.co.uk/news/world-asia-61413335 [accessed 18/05/22].

90 Salvatore Cernuzio, "Cardinal Zen arrested in Hong Kong, Holy See expresses concern", *Vatican News,* 11th May 2022 https://www.vaticannews.va/en/pope/news/2022-05/cardinal-zen-arrested-in-hong-kong-holy-see-expresses-concern.html [accessed 18/05/22].

91 Torode, "Vatican envoy in Hong Kong warns Catholic missions to prepare for China crackdown", Reuters, op. cit.

92 "Catholic Diocese of Hong Kong faces shortage of Chinese Bible due to unwillingness of mainland Chinese printing houses", *ChinaAid,* 1st August 2022 https://www.chinaaid.org/2022/08/catholic-diocese-of-hong-kong-faces.html [accessed 12/08/22].

93 USCIRF, *2022 Annual Report,* p. 50.

94 "Egyptian President Affirms Church Building in Every New City", *International Christian Concern,* 14th March 2022 https://www.persecution.org/2022/03/14/egyptian-president-affirms-church-building-every-new-city/ [accessed 05/05/22].

95 "The number of legally recognized Christian churches rises to 1738," *Agenzia Fides,* 20th October 2020 www.fides.org/en/news/68865-AFRICA_EGYPT_The_number_of_legally_recognized_Christian_churches_rises_to_1738 [accessed 30/11/20].

96 "239 Churches and Places of Worship legalised by Government Committee", *CSW,* 27th April 2022.

97 Ibid.

98 John Pontifex, John Newton and Fionn Shiner, *Hear Her Cries: The kidnapping, forced conversion and sexual victimisation of Christian women and girls* (London: ACN (UK), 2021), pp. 12ff.

99 John Newton (original interview by André Stiefenhofer), "Fresh plea to help abused Christian girls", *ACN (UK) News,* 20th January 2022 https://acnuk.org/news/egypt-international-fresh-plea-to-help-abused-christian-girls/ [accessed 05/05/22].

100 Indeed, this material is usually posted in Arabic, making it difficult for English-speaking organisations to monitor the cases that do appear on social media.

101 "Egypt: ex-kidnapper admits 'they get paid for every Coptic Christian girl they bring in'", *World Watch Monitor,* 14th September 2017 https://www.worldwatchmonitor.org/2017/09/egypt-ex-kidnapper-admits-get-paid-every-copt-christian-girl-bring/ [accessed 05/05/22].

102 Newton, "Fresh plea to help abused Christian girls", *ACN (UK) News,* op. cit.

103 "Apostasy and Blasphemy Laws in Egypt", *Coptic Solidarity,* 9th March 2020 https://www.copticsolidarity.org/2020/03/09/apostasy-and-blasphemy-laws-in-egypt/ [accessed 05/05/22]

104 "Egypt cracks down on blasphemy in wave of arrests," *Al-Monitor,* 20th November 2020 https://www.al-monitor.com/pulse/originals/2020/11/egypt-arrests-christians-muslims-insulting-religion.html [accessed 05/05/22].

105 USCIRF, *2022 Annual Report,* p. 50.

106 "Egypt cracks down on blasphemy in wave of arrests," Al-Monitor, op. cit; "Christians, others in Egypt arrested for 'insulting Islam'," *Morning Star News,* 23rd November 2020 https://morningstarnews.org/2020/11/christians-others-in-egypt-arrested-for-insulting-islam/ [both sites accessed 05/05/22].

107 "Shops and homes of Coptic Christians ransacked and set on fire in sectarian attacks in the village of al Barsha", *Agenzia Fides,* 27th November 2020 www.fides.org/en/news/69122 [accessed 05/05/22]; "Christian's Detention Extended", *CSW,* 15th September 2021.

108 *Hear Her Cries,* p 15.

109 "ISIL-linked group in Egypt claims execution of Copt, 2 tribesmen", *Al Jazeera,* 19th April 2021 https://www.aljazeera.com/news/2021/4/19/isil-linked-group-in-egypt-claims-execution-of-copt-2-others ; Basma Mostafa, "Family of murdered Coptic man forced to leave North Sinai, faced online threats", *Mada,* 26th May 2021 https://www.madamasr.com/en/2021/05/26/news/politics/family-of-murdered-coptic-man-forced-to-leave-north-sinai-after-continued-threats/ [Both sites accessed 04/05/22].

110 "Local Authorities confiscate land belonging to Monastery", *CSW,* 4th June 2021; Michael Girgis, "Coptic Church issues statement on crisis at Wadi al-Rayan Monastery", *Watani,* 31st May 2021 https://en.wataninet.com/coptic-affairs-coptic-affairs/coptic-affairs/coptic-church-issues-statement-on-crisis-at-wadi-al-rayan-monastery/35483/ [accessed 05/05/22].

111 *Hear Her Cries,* p 15.

112 "Christian's Detention Extended", *CSW,* 15th September 2021.

113 "Egyptian Christian Students Persecuted in Teacher-Led Incident", *International Christian Concern*, 18th November 2021 https://www.persecution.org/2021/11/18/egyptian-christian-students-persecuted-teacher-led-incident/ [accessed 04/05/22].

114 Kevin J. Jones, "Months later, nine Egyptian Christians still detained after protests to rebuild church", *CNA*, 5th April 2022 https://www.catholicnewsagency.com/news/250896/months-later-nine-egyptian-christians-still-detained-after-protests-to-rebuild-church [accessed 28/04/22].

115 "Coptic Priest Fatally Stabbed on Egyptian Street", *International Christian Concern*, 8th April 2022 https://www.persecution.org/2022/04/08/coptic-priest-fatally-stabbed-egyptian-street/ [accessed 04/05/22]; "Coptic Orthodox priest fatally stabbed", *Independent Catholic News*, 12th April 2022 https://www.indcatholicnews.com/news/44459 [accessed 04/05/22]; "Murdered Egyptian Priest Faced Years of Persecution Prior to His Death", *International Christian Concern*, 12th April 2022 https://www.persecution.org/2022/04/12/murdered-egyptian-priest-faced-years-persecution-prior-death/ [accessed 04/05/22]; Arnold Neliba, "Suspect Convicted to Death Penalty for Murder of Coptic Priest", *CISA*, 20th May 2022 http://cisanewsafrica.com/egypt-suspect-convicted-to-death-penalty-for-murder-of-coptic-priest/ [accessed 25/05/22].

116 "Coptic Woman Slapped and Verbally Assaulted by Muslim Man", *International Christian Concern*, 3rd May 2022 https://www.persecution.org/2022/05/03/coptic-woman-slapped-verbally-assaulted-muslim-man/ [accessed 04/05/22].

117 "Prosecution charges killer of Sohag Copt with intentional murder", *Watani International*, 10th June 2022 https://en.wataninet.com/news-2/crime/prosecution-charges-killer-of-sohag-copt-with-intentional-murder/38890/ [accessed 16/06/22].

118 Anugrah Kumar, "Mobs attack Christians' homes, businesses after church's legal recognition", *Christian Post*, 16th July 2022 https://www.christianpost.com/news/mobs-attack-christian-homes-after-churchs-legal-recognition.html [accessed 21/07/22].

119 "Christian father and son hospitalised following knife attack", *CSW*, 1st August 2022.

120 "Two Copts shot dead in Sinai by Islamist jihadis", *Watani*, 30th August 2022 https://en.wataninet.com/coptic-affairs-coptic-affairs/coptic-affairs/two-copts-shot-dead-in-sinai-by-islamist-jihadis/39580/ [accessed 15/09/22].

121 Mohy Omer, "Religious Freedom Conditions in Eritrea", *USCIRF*, August 2021 https://www.uscirf.gov/sites/default/files/2021-08/2021%20Eritrea%20Policy%20Update_0.pdf [accessed 13/05/22].

122 Ibid.

123 US State Dept., "Eritrea", *2020 Report on International Religious Freedom* https://www.state.gov/reports/2020-report-on-international-religious-freedom/eritrea/ [accessed 13/05/22].

124 Ibid.

125 Omer, "Religious Freedom Conditions in Eritrea", *USCIRF*, op. cit.

126 "Two elderly pastors imprisoned for their faith", *International Institute for Religious Freedom*, 15th September 2021 https://www.iirf.eu/news/other-news/two-elderly-pastors-imprisoned-for-their-faith/ [accessed 13/05/22].

127 Omer, "Religious Freedom Conditions in Eritrea", *USCIRF*, op. cit.

128 Ibid.

129 "Eritrea: Bishops criticise the nationalisation of Catholic schools", *Vatican News*, 10th June 2021 https://www.vaticannews.va/en/africa/news/2021-06/eritrea-bishops-criticise-the-nationalisation-of-catholic-schoo.html [accessed 13/05/22].

130 John Pontifex, "Sick forced from beds as 21 hospitals and clinics forced to shut", *ACN (UK) News*, 20th June 2019 https://acnuk.org/news/eritrea-sick-forced-from-beds-as-21-hospitals-and-clinics-forced-to-shut/ [accessed 13/05/22].

131 "Catholic Nuns evicted from health centres", *CSW*, 5th July 2019 https://www.csw.org.uk/2019/07/05/press/4404/article.htm [accessed 16/05/22].

132 "Eritrean bishops says seizure of Catholic schools is 'hatred against the faith'", *The Catholic World Report*, 17th September 2019 https://www.catholicworldreport.com/2019/09/17/eritrean-bishops-say-seizure-of-catholic-schools-is-hatred-against-the-faith/ [accessed 13/05/22].

133 John Newton, "Patriarch dies in captivity", *ACN (UK) News*, 11th February 2022 https://acnuk.org/news/eritrea-patriarch-dies-in-captivity/ [accessed 09/05/22].

134 Ibid.

135 Omer, "Religious Freedom Conditions in Eritrea", *USCIRF*, op. cit.

136 "Five Christians arrested after 69 released", *Church in Chains*, 6th October 2020 https://www.churchinchains.ie/news-by-country/sub-saharan-africa/eritrea/eritrea-five-christians-arrested-after-69-released/ [accessed 09/05/22].

137 "Religious freedom hopes dashes in Eritrea as 35 more Christians arrested", *Release International*, 31st March 2021 https://releaseinternational.org/religious-freedom-hopes-dashed-in-eritrea-as-35-more-christians-arrested/ [accessed 09/05/22].

138 Ibid.

139 Omer, "Religious Freedom Conditions in Eritrea", *USCIRF*, op. cit.

140 "Eritrea: Bishops criticise the nationalisation of Catholic schools", *Vatican News*, 10th June 2021 https://www.vaticannews.va/en/africa/news/2021-06/eritrea-bishops-criticise-the-nationalisation-of-catholic-schoo.html [accessed 13/05/22].

141 "Three elderly pastors arrested", *Church in Chains*, 5th August 2021 https://www.churchinchains.ie/news-by-country/sub-saharan-africa/eritrea/eritrea-three-elderly-pastors-arrested/ [accessed 09/05/22].

142 "15 Christians re-arrested", *Release International*, 20th September 2021 https://releaseinternational.org/eritrea-15-christians-re-arrested/ [accessed 09/05/22].

143 Newton, "Patriarch dies in captivity", *ACN (UK) News*, op. cit

144 "Twenty-nine Christians arrested at prayer meeting", *Church in Chains*, 22nd March 2022 https://www.churchinchains.ie/news-by-country/sub-saharan-africa/eritrea/eritrea-twenty-nine-christians-arrested-at-prayer-meeting/ [accessed 09/05/22].

145 Fredrick Nzwili, "Eritrean government rounds up teens from church service", *Crux*, 8th September 2022 https://cruxnow.com/church-in-africa/2022/09/eritrean-government-rounds-up-teens-from-church-service [accessed 21/09/22].

146 Fionn Shiner, "Surge in violence leads to up to 1,000 deaths", *ACN (UK) News*, 22nd January 2021 https://acnuk.org/news/ethiopia-surge-in-violence-leads-to-up-to-1000-deaths/ [accessed 30/05/22].

147 Jane Flanagan, "Ancient monastery 'looted and bombed' in Ethiopia'", *The Times*, 16th February 2021 https://www.thetimes.co.uk/article/monastery-bombed-and-looted-in-ethiopian-war-rzg2crrc3 ; Duarte Mendonca, "Ethiopian Orthodox Church Patriarch condemns Tigray 'genocide'", *CNN*, 8th May 2021 https://edition.cnn.com/2021/05/08/africa/orthodox-church-tigray-ethiopia-intl/index.html [all sites accessed 30/05/22].

148 Fasikaw Menberu and Farouk Chothia, "Ethiopia Tigray crisis: From monk to soldier – how war has split a

church", *BBC News*, 3rd October 2021 https://www.bbc.co.uk/news/world-africa-58742178 [accessed 30/05/22].

149 Jason Burke, "Ethiopia: 1,900 people killed in massacres in Tigray identified", *Guardian*, 2nd April 2021 https://www.theguardian.com/world/2021/apr/02/ethiopia-1900-people-killed-in-massacres-in-tigray-identified [accessed 25/07/22].

150 Fionn Shiner, "Surge in violence leads to up to 1,000 deaths", *ACN (UK) News*, op. cit.; "Ethiopia: Eritrean troops' massacre of hundreds of Axum civilians may amount to crime against humanity", *Amnesty International*, 26th February 2021 https://www.amnesty.org/en/latest/news/2021/02/ethiopia-eritrean-troops-massacre-of-hundreds-of-axum-civilians-may-amount-to-crime-against-humanity/ [accessed 30/05/22].; "Ethiopia's Tigray crisis: How a massacre in the sacred city of Aksum unfolded", *BBC News*, 26th February 2021 https://www.bbc.co.uk/news/world-africa-56198469 [accessed 31/05/22]; "Ethiopia's Tigray crisis: How a massacre in the sacred city of Aksum unfolded", *BBC News*, 26th February 2021 https://www.bbc.co.uk/news/world-africa-56198469 [accessed 09/08/22].

151 Fionn Shiner, "'Genocide is happening in Tigray'", *ACN (UK) News*, 28th May 2021 https://acnuk.org/news/ethiopia-genocide-is-happening-in-tigray/ [accessed 30/05/22]; Burke, "Ethiopia: 1,900 people killed in massacres in Tigray identified", *The Guardian*, op. cit.

152 Flanagan, "Ancient monastery 'looted and bombed' in Ethiopia'", *The Times*, op. cit.

153 Shiner, "'Genocide is happening in Tigray'", *ACN (UK) News*, op. cit.

154 "Tigray Church denounces conflict, loss of lives in Ethiopian region", *Vatican News*, 21st January 2022 https://www.vaticannews.va/en/church/news/2022-01/ethiopia-tigray-adigrat-diocese-conflict-humanitarian-crisis.html [accessed 31/05/22].

155 "Catholic Eparchy Adigrat: Humanitarian Aid to Save Millions of People Dying from Merciless Man-made Famine in Tigray", *Tghat*, 6th April 2022 https://www.tghat.com/2022/04/06/catholic-eparchy-adigrat-humanitarian-aid-to-save-millions-of-people-dying-from-merciless-man-made-famine-in-tigray/ [accessed 31/05/22].

156 Silar Isenjia, "Cardinal in Ethiopia Says Humanitarian Situation in Tigray Worsening, Suffering Increasing", *ACI Africa*, 20th April 2022 https://www.aciafrica.org/news/5692/cardinal-in-ethiopia-says-humanitarian-situation-in-tigray-worsening-suffering-increasing [accessed 01/06/22].

157 Fionn Shiner, "Surge in violence leads to up to 1,000 deaths", *ACN (UK) News*, op. cit.

158 "Ethiopia: Eritrean troops' massacre of hundreds of Axum civilians may amount to crime against humanity", *Amnesty International*, op. cit.

159 Jane Flanagan, "Ancient monastery 'looted and bombed' in Ethiopia'", *The Times*, op. cit.

160 Maria Lozano and Fionn Shiner, "'The people are traumatised'", *ACN (UK) News*, 27th April 2021 https://acnuk.org/news/ethiopia-the-people-are-traumatised/ [accessed 30/05/22].

161 Duarte Mendonca, "Ethiopian Orthodox Church Patriarch condemns Tigray 'genocide'", *CNN*, 8th May 2021 https://edition.cnn.com/2021/05/08/africa/orthodox-church-tigray-ethiopia-intl/index.html [accessed 30/05/22].

162 Shiner, "'Genocide is happening in Tigray'", *ACN (UK) News*, op. cit.

163 Fasikaw Menberu and Farouk Chothia, "Ethiopia Tigray crisis: From monk to soldier – how war has split a church", *BBC News*, op. cit.

164 "Voices from Tigray: Brutalities against Religious Leaders, Holy Places and Heritage in Tigray", *EEPA*,

8th June 2021 https://www.eepa.be/wp-content/uploads/2021/05/7_Voices-from-Tigray-Testimony-by-a-Tigray-Priest-in-East-Africa.docx.pdf [accessed 30/05/22].

165 https://twitter.com/tghatmedia/status/14485933017209937927?s=21&t=dujSThDBncljTSIkWEUoRg

166 "Christian priests targeted in Tigray", *Release International*, 1st November 2021 https://releaseinternational.org/christian-priests-targeted-in-tigray/ [accessed 27/07/22].

167 Fredrick Nzwili, "Nuns and priests flee, more churches shut in Ethiopia's Tigray region", *Crux*, 4th August 2022 https://cruxnow.com/cns/2022/08/nuns-and-priests-flee-more-churches-shut-in-ethiopias-tigray-region [accessed 09/08/22].

168 Ibid.

169 "Violence against churches and Christians increase: United Christian Forum appeals to authorities", *Asianews*, 13th June 2022 http://www.fides.org/en/news/72348-ASIA_INDIA_Violence_against_churches_and_Christians_increase_United_Christian_Forum_appeals_to_authorities ; Santosh Digal, *Radio Veritas Asia*, 15th February, 2022 https://www.rvasia.org/church-asia/53-cases-violence-against-christians-45-days-reported-india ; "There were over 300 attacks on Christians in India till July this year", *GTN News*, 7th September 2022 https://geotvnews.com/there-were-over-300-attacks-on-christians-in-india-till-july-this-year-ngo-gtn-news/ [all sites accessed 16/09/22].

170 *Federation of Indian American Christian Organizations of North America Annual Report 2022*, p. 4.

171 Devendra Pratap Singh Shekhawat, "Police and Govt Ally With Hindu Groups Intimidating, Attacking Christians In MP, 0.29% Of State Population", *Article 14*, 3rd February 2022 https://www.article-14.com/post/police-govt-ally-with-hindu-groups-intimidating-attacking-christians-in-mp-0-29-of-state-population--61fb458cf16f5 [accessed 10/05/22].

172 Jeffrey Gettleman and Suhasini Raj, "Arrests, beatings and secret prayers: Inside the persecution of India's Christians, *New York Times*, [22nd December 2021] https://www.nytimes.com/2021/12/22/world/asia/india-christians-attacked.html [accessed 01/03/22].

173 "Persecution Escalates in India as 30 Christians Jailed", *International Christian Concern*, 2nd June 2022 https://www.persecution.org/2022/06/02/persecution-escalates-india-30-christians-jailed/ [accessed 16/06/22].

174 "2021 'the most violent year' for Christians in India", *Agenzia Fides*, 4th January 2022 http://www.fides.org/en/news/71399-ASIA_INDIA_2021_the_most_violent_year_for_Christians_in_India [accessed 03/03/22].

175 Alishan Jafri, "Hate Watch: In Presence of BJP Bigwigs, Chhattisgarh Hindutva Leader Calls for Beheading Minorities", *The Wire*, 21st October 2021 https://thewire.in/communalism/chhattisgarh-hindutva-leader-christian-bjp-leaders-hate-watch [accessed 03/03/22].

176 Neel Madhav and Alishan Jafri, "Why India is witnessing spike in attacks on, Christians, churches", *Al Jazeera*, 2nd December 2021 https://www.aljazeera.com/news/2021/12/2/india-christians-church-hindu-groups-bjp-conversion [accessed 17/06/22].

177 "Jail term, fine for 'illegal' conversions in Uttar Pradesh", *The Hindu*, 24th November 2020 https://www.thehindu.com/news/national/uttar-pradesh-cabinet-clears-ordinance-against-love-jihad/article33170627.ece 03/03/22 ; *USCIRF*, "India", *Annual Report 2021* https://www.uscirf.gov/sites/default/files/2021-05/India%20Chapter%20AR2021.pdf [accessed 03/03/22]; "What UP govt's new anti-conversion law says, and origin of 'love jihad'", *The Print*, 26th November 2020 https://theprint.in/opinion/what-up-govts-new-anti-

conversion-law-says-and-origin-of-love-jihad/552115/ [accessed 03/03/22].

178 Gettleman and Raj, "Arrests, beatings and secret prayers: Inside the persecution of India's Christians", *New York Times*, op. cit.

179 "Police Beat Christians in Custody in Uttar Pradesh, India", *Christian News Now*, 12th October 2021 https://christiannewsnow.com/police-beat-christians-in-custody-in-uttar-pradesh-india/ [accessed 09/03/22]

180 Bobins Abraham, "Install Idol of Goddess Saraswati on the Campus, Christian School in MP's Satna gets ultimatum", *India Times*, 27th October, 2021 https://www.indiatimes.com/news/india/install-idol-of-goddess-saraswati-on-the-campus-christian-school-in-mps-satna-gets-ultimatum-552649.html [accessed 03/02/22].

181 Alishan Jafri, "Hate Watch: In Presence of BJP Bigwigs, Chhattisgarh Hindutva Leader Calls for Beheading Minorities", *The Wire*, 21st October 2021 https://thewire.in/communalism/chhattisgarh-hindutva-leader-christian-bjp-leaders-hate-watch [accessed 03/03/22].

182 M S Sreeja, "In Karnataka, Right-Wing Groups set Christian Religious Books on fire", *NDTV*, 12th December 2021 https://www.ndtv.com/india-news/in-karnataka-right-wing-activists-set-christian-religious-books-on-fire-2647730 [accessed 03/03/22].

183 "Catholic school in India attacked by Hindu mob", *Vatican News*, 7th December 2021 https://www.vaticannews.va/en/church/news/2021-12/india-catholic-school-attacked-hindu.html ; Fionn Shiner, "Christians in India seek protection from Hindutva government", *ACN (UK) News*, 14th December 2021 https://acnuk.org/news/india-christians-in-india-seek-protection-from-hindutva-government/ *[both sites accessed 11/08/22].*

184 "Hindu outfit activists burn Santa Claus effigies in Agra", *The Hindu*, 26th December 2021 https://www.thehindu.com/news/national/other-states/hindu-outfit-activists-burn-santa-claus-effigies-in-agra/article38040645.ece [accessed 03/03/22].

185 "Mob of 200 Attacks House Church in Central India", *International Christian Concern*, 13th January https://www.persecution.org/2022/01/13/mob-200-attacks-house-church-central-india/ [accessed 09/03/22].

186 Anugrah Kumar, "Christians in India say police officer who burned down their church is threatening to kill them", *Christian Post*, 21st May 2022 https://www.christianpost.com/news/india-christians-say-police-officer-burned-down-church-threatened-murder.html ; "Christians Accuse Policeman in India of Destroying Church Building". *Morning Star News*, 19th May 2022 https://morningstarnews.org/2022/05/christians-accuse-policeman-in-india-of-destroying-church-building/ [accessed 08/07/22].

187 "Christians hold silent protest against anti-conversion Bill", *The Hindu*, 3rd March 2022 https://www.thehindu.com/news/cities/Mangalore/christians-hold-silent-protest-against-anti-conversion-bill/article65187298.ece ; "Mangalore: Why was the 40-year-old St. Antony Holy Cross prayer hall demolished?", *Sab Rang*, 7th February 2022 https://sabrangindia.in/article/mangalore-why-was-40-year-old-st-antony-holy-cross-prayer-hall-demolished ; "Karnataka: What is the message sent by demolishing 18-year-old Jesus statue?", *Sab Rang*, 14th Febryary 2022 https://sabrangindia.in/article/karnataka-what-message-sent-demolishing-18-year-old-jesus-statue [all sites accessed 08/03/22].

188 Nirmala Carvalho, "Christian pastor murdered in India after threats from Hindu nationalists", *Crux*, 30th March https://cruxnow.com/church-in-asia/2022/03/christian-pastor-murdered-in-india-after-threats-from-hindu-nationalists [accessed 30/03/22].

189 Nirmala Carvalho, "Hindu nationalists want Christian chaplains banned from Indian jails", *Crux*, 13th April 2022 https://cruxnow.com/church-in-asia/2022/04/hindu-nationalist-want-christian-chaplains-banned-from-indian-jails [accessed 14/04/22].

190 "26 arrested for illegal conversion in Fatehpur", *Times of India*, 16th April 2022 http://timesofindia.indiatimes.com/articleshow/90870723.cms ; "26 Christians including hospital staff and a Pastor arrested under false forced conversions charges", *British Asian Christian Association*, 18th April 2022 https://www.britishasianchristians.org/baca-news/26-christians-arrested/ ; "Indian Christians arrested for attending Maundy Thursday service", *UCA News*, 20th April 2022 https://www.UCA News.com/news/indian-christians-arrested-for-attending-maundy-thursday-service/96954 [all sites accessed 10/05/22].

191 "Violence against churches and Christians increase: United Christian Forum appeals to authorities", *Asianews*, 13th June 2022 http://www.fides.org/en/news/72348-ASIA_INDIA_Violence_against_churches_and_Christians_increase_United_Christian_Forum_appeals_to_authorities [accessed 15/06/22]

192 US State Dept., "Iran", 2020 Report on International Religious Freedom https://www.state.gov/reports/2020-report-on-international-religious-freedom/iran/ [accessed 26/05/22].

193 Ibid.

194 Ibid.

195 Ibid.

196 Ibid.

197 US State Dept., "Iran", *2021 Report on International Religious Freedom* https://www.state.gov/reports/2021-report-on-international-religious-freedom/iran/ [accessed 23/06/22].

198 Ibid.

199 US State Dept., "Iran", *2020*, op. cit.

200 Ibid.

201 Christopher Summers, "Iranian couple has daughter taken from them – just because they follow Jesus", *Open Doors (USA)*, 30th September 2020 https://www.opendoorsusa.org/christian-persecution/stories/iranian-couple-has-daughter-taken-from-them-just-because-they-follow-jesus/ [accessed 26/05/22].

202 Ibid.

203 USCIRF, "Iran", *2022 Annual Report* https://www.uscirf.gov/sites/default/files/2022-04/2022%20USCIRF%20Annual%20Report_1.pdf [accessed 26/05/22].

204 Ibid.

205 "Four Christian converts arrested in Dezful, others interrogated", *Article18*, 21st April 2022 https://articleeighteen.com/news/8394/ [accessed 23/06/22].

206 US State Dept., "Iran", *2022*, op. cit.

207 "Christians in Karaj ordered to stop meeting", *CSW*, 5th February 2021 April 2022 https://www.csw.org.uk/2021/02/05/press/4971/article.htm [accessed 25/05/22].

208 "Four Christian converts arrested in Dezful, others interrogated", *Article18*, 21st April 2021 https://articleeighteen.com/news/8394/ [accessed 15/08/22].

209 "Christian stand trial under new amendment to the Iranian penal code", *CSW*, 23rd June 2021 https://www.csw.org.uk/2021/06/23/press/5308/article.htm [accessed 26/05/22].

210 "Three Christians have prison sentences reduced", *CSW*, 1st September 2021 https://www.csw.org.uk/2021/09/01/press/5387/article.htm [accessed 26/05/22].

211 "Pastor re-arrested two weeks after release", *CSW*, 19th January 2022 https://www.csw.org.uk/2022/01/19/press/5551/article.htm [accessed 26/05/22].

212 Ibid.
213 "Three Christians have prison sentences reduced", *CSW*, op. cit.
214 "Converts cleared of any crime must now attend 're-education' classes", *Article18*, 1st February 2022 https://articleeighteen.com/news/10283/ [accessed 15/08/22].
215 Ostanwire, "Two Christians Converts Summoned to Prison", *IranWire*, 17th February 2022 https://iranwire.com/en/religious-minorities/71325 [accessed 25/05/22].
216 Samuel Smith, "Iran acquits 9 Christian converts of 'acting against national security' in 'landmark decision'", *Christian Post*, 3rd March 2022 https://www.christianpost.com/news/iran-acquits-christian-converts-landmark-decision.html [accessed 25/05/22].
217 "Iranian pastor granted temporary furlough from prison", *CSW*, 13th April 2022 https://www.csw.org.uk/2022/04/13/press/5679/article.htm [accessed 26/05/22].
218 "Three Christians Given Harsh Sentences by Iran Revolutionary Court", *Iran International*, 6th May 2022 https://www.iranintl.com/en/202205062760 [accessed 15/08/22].
219 USCIRF, "Iraq", *2022 Annual Report*, p. 54 https://www.uscirf.gov/sites/default/files/2022-04/2022%20USCIRF%20Annual%20Report_1.pdf [accessed 20/06/22].
220 Cole Bunzel, "Explainer: The Islamic State in 2021", *Wilson Center*, 10th December 2021 https://www.wilsoncenter.org/article/explainer-islamic-state-2021 [accessed 20/06/22].
221 Ibid.
222 John Pontifex, "The Christians working to resurrect a future in Iraq", *Tablet*, 14th April 2022 https://www.thetablet.co.uk/features/2/21761/the-christians-working-to-resurrect-a-future-in-iraq [accessed 20/06/22].
223 "Situation of Christians in Baghdad", *UNHCR*, p.2 https://www.refworld.org/pdfid/5a66f80e4.pdf [accessed 22/06/22].
224 Ashish Kumar Sen, "Unemployment Replaces ISIS as Top Security Concern for Minorities in Iraq", *United States Institute of Peace*, 22nd June 2022 https://www.usip.org/publications/2021/06/unemployment-replaces-isis-top-security-concern-minorities-iraq [accessed 22/06/22].
225 USCIRF, "Iraq", *2022*, op. cit.
226 Pontifex, "The Christians working to resurrect a future in Iraq", *Tablet*, op. cit.
227 ACN project-assessment trip to Iraq, March 2022.
228 "ASIA/IRAQ – President of Iraq informs Patriarchs: I have invited the Pope to pray together in memory of Abraham", *Agenzia fides*, 29th November 2018 http://www.fides.org/en/news/65176-ASIA_IRAQ_President_of_Iraq_informs_Patriarchs_I_have_invited_the_Pope_to_pray_together_in_memory_of_Abraham [accessed 20/06/22].
229 Bunzel, "Explainer: The Islamic State in 2021", *Wilson Center*, op. cit.
230 ACN, "Iraq", *Religious Freedom in the World Report 2021* https://acninternational.org/religiousfreedomreport/reports/iq/#endnote-1 [accessed 22/06/22].
231 "Kurdistan, Christian villages hit by Turkish raids against the PKK (VIDEO)", *Asianews*, 15th September 2020 http://www.Asianews.it/news-en/Kurdistan-Christian-villages-hit-by-Turkish-raids-against-the-PKK-(VIDEO)-51036.html [accessed 24/06/22].
232 "Iraq 2005", *Constitute*, https://www.constituteproject.org/constitution/Iraq_2005?lang=en. [accessed 20/06/22].
233 "Patriarch Sako to the Government: A Law on Personal Status is needed that respects the identity of Christians", *Holy Land Christian Ecumenical Foundation*, 21st July 2020 https://hcef.org/790818356-asia-iraq-patriarch-sako-to-the-government-a-law-on-personal-status-is-needed-that-respects-the-identity-of-christians/ [accessed 20/06/22].
234 Elise Ann Allen, "Iraqi parliament formally declares Christmas a national holiday", *Crux*, 18th December 2020 https://cruxnow.com/church-in-the-middle-east/2020/12/iraqi-parliament-formally-declares-christmas-a-national-holiday [accessed 20/06/22].
235 "The visit of Pope Francis to Iraq raises many questions," *Middle East Monitor*, 9th March 2021 https://www.middleeastmonitor.com/20210309-the-visit-of-pope-francis-to-iraq-raises-many-questions/ [accessed 25/06/22].
236 Allen, "Iraqi parliament formally declares Christmas a national holiday", *Crux*, op. cit.
237 "A Moment of Fraternity: Recalling Pope Francis' visit to Iraq," *Vatican News*, 3rd June 2021 https://www.vaticannews.va/en/world/news/2021-06/a-moment-of-fraternity-recalling-pope-francis-visit-to-iraq.html [accessed 25/06/22].
238 "Al-Kadhimi declares the 6th of March a national day for tolerance and coexistence", *Shafaq*, 6th March 2021 https://shafaq.com/en/Iraq-News/Al-Kadhimi-declares-the-6th-of-March-a-national-day-for-tolerance-and-coexistence [accessed 26/06/22].
239 Allen, "Iraqi patriarch calls for religious pluralism amid political deadlock", *Crux*, op. cit.
240 Kurdistan: Christian suburb of Ankawa becomes a district with full powers", *Asianews*, 10th June 2021 https://www.Asianews.it/news-en/Kurdistan:-Christian-suburb-of-Ankawa-becomes-a-district-with-full-powers-54219.html [accessed 22/06/22].
241 "USCIRF Praises Additional Humanitarian Assistance to Iraqis Displaced by ISIS", *USCIRF*, 28th June 2021 https://www.uscirf.gov/news-room/releases-statements/uscirf-praises-additional-humanitarian-assistance-iraqis-displaced [accessed 27/06/22].
242 "Attack on Iraqi Christian Home Sparks Insecurity Fear", *International Christian Concern*, 12th January 2021 https://www.persecution.org/2021/12/01/attack-iraqi-christian-home-sparks-insecurity-fear/ [accessed: 27/06/22].
243 Farhad Rezaei, "The Invisible Jihad: The treatment of Christinas by Iran Proxies," *Philos Project*, June 2022, p.3 https://philosproject.org/wp-content/uploads/2022/06/Invisible-Jihad-Report.pdf [accessed: 27/06/22].
244 Lisa Zengarini, "Cardinal Sako Warns Christians in Iraq Risk Disappearing", *Vatican News*, 24th August 2022 https://www.vaticannews.va/en/church/news/2022-08/cardinal-sako-warns-christians-in-iraq-risk-disappearing.html [accessed 16/09/22].
245 Catholic University in Erbil Scholarship Programme https://cue.edu.krd/scholarship/ [accessed 25/07/22].
246 John Pontifex, "Joudy, 18: Daring to dream", *Miracles Do Happen* (London: ACN UK, June 2022) https://acnuk.org/wp-content/uploads/2022/06/Iraq-2022-6pp-Report-WEB.pdf [accessed 25/07/22]
247 Patriarchs and heads of local Churches in Jerusalem, *Statement on the Current Threat to the Christian Presence in the Holy Land*, 13th December https://j-diocese.org/wordpress/2021/12/14/statement-on-the-current-threat-to-the-christian-presence-in-the-holy-land/ [accessed 12/05/22].
248 Stuart Winer, "Jerusalem church leaders: 'Radical' Israeli groups driving Christians from Holy Land", *Times of Israel*, 19th December 2021 https://www.timesofisrael.com/jerusalem-church-leaders-warn-radical-groups-driving-christians-from-holy-land/ [accessed 10/05/22].
249 Chaim Levinson, "Israeli Extremist Group Leader Calls for Torching of Churches", *Haaretz*, 6th August 2015 https://www.haaretz.com/.premium-israeli-extremist-group-leader-calls-for-torching-of-churches-1.5383670 [accessed 12/05/22].
250 Nir Hasson and Jack Khoury, "Jerusalem Man Arrested for Arson at One of Christianity's Holiest Sites", *Haaretz*, 5th

December 2020 https://www.haaretz.com/israel-news/. premium-church-of-all-nations-in-jerusalem-arson-christianity-holiest-sites-1.9349115 [accessed 10/05/22].

251 "Christian church in Jerusalem attacked for 4th time in 1 month", *Daily Sabah*, 2nd March 2021 https://www. dailysabah.com/world/mid-east/christian-church-in-jerusalem-attacked-for-4th-time-in-1-month [accessed 12/05/22].

252 Courtney Mares, "Vandals steal cross from altar of Catholic church in the Holy Land", *CNA*, 23rd August 2021 https://www.catholicnewsagency.com/news/248746/ vandals-steal-cross-from-altar-of-catholic-church-in-the-holy-land [accessed 12/05/22].

253 Judith Sudilovsky, "Israel's decision to cancel cultural event upsets Catholic leaders", *National Catholic Reporter*, 29th October 2021 https://www.ncronline.org/ news/politics/israels-decision-cancel-cultural-event-upsets-catholic-leaders ; "Catholic Ordinaries condemn Israeli decision to cancel event at Abraham's House in Jerusalem", *Latin Patriarchate of Jerusalem*, 28th October 2021 https://www.lpj.org/posts/catholic-ordinaries-condemn-israeli-decision-to-cancel-event-at-abraham-s-house-in-jerusalem.html [both sites accessed 17/05/22].

254 Jacob Magid, "Parks authority says it's shelving Mount of Olives plan that angered church leaders", *Times of Israel*, 21st February 2022 https://www.timesofisrael. com/parks-authority-says-its-shelving-mount-of-olives-plan-that-angered-church-leaders/ ; "Park plan on Mount of Olives suspended after Churches' protest", *Vatican News*, 22nd February 2022 https://www. vaticannews.va/en/church/news/2022-02/park-plan-on-mount-of-olives-suspended-after-churches-protest. html [accessed 15/06/22].

255 Dario Salvi, "Little Petra Hotel affair: The fate of Christians in Jerusalem on the line", *Asianews*, 5th April 2022 http://www.Asianews.it/news-en/Little-Petra-Hotel-affair:-The-fate-of-Christians-in-Jerusalem-on-the-line-55520.html [accessed 12/05/22].

256 Emily Jones, "Palestinian Pastor released after being jailed for meeting with Israeli Leader", *CBN News*, 11th April 2022 https://www1.cbn.com/cbnnews/Israel/2022/ april/palestinian-pastor-released-after-being-jailed-for-meeting-with-israeli-leader [accessed 14/04/22].

257 Joseph Krauss, "Israeli restrictions on 'Holy Fire' ignite Christian outrage", *ABC News*, 23rd April 2022 https:// abcnews.go.com/International/wireStory/israeli-restrictions-holy-fire-ignite-christian-outrage-84260378 [accessed 12/05/22].

258 John Newton, "Catholic leaders condemn police brutality at funeral", *ACN (UK) News*, 17th May 2022 https://acnuk.org/news/holy-land-catholic-leaders-condemn-police-brutality-at-funeral/ ; Kareem Khadder and Celine Alkhaldi, "Al Jazeera journalist Shireen Abu Akleh's brother slams violent actions of Israeli police at her funeral", *CNN*, 16th May 2022 https://edition. cnn.com/2022/05/16/middleeast/shireen-abu-akleh-brother-police-criticism-intl/index.html [both sites accessed 17/05/22].

259 "The Patriarchate of Jerusalem was targeted by extremists", *Orthodox Times*, 7th June 2022 https:// orthodoxtimes.com/the-patriarchate-of-jerusalem-was-targeted-by-extremists/ ; "Jerusalem's Greek Orthodox patriarchate denounces transgressions by Israeli extremists on its property", *Wafa*, 6th June 2022 https://english.wafa.ps/Pages/Details/129559 [both sites accessed 08/06/22].

260 "Seeking Justice and Peace for All in the Middle East", *Statement of the WCC 11th Assembly in Karlsruhe, Germany*, 8th September 2022 https://www.oikoumene. org/resources/documents/seeking-justice-and-peace-for-all-in-the-middle-east [accessed 26/09/22].

261 "Maldives: a paradise for tourism where Christians are persecuted", *European Post*, http://europeanpost.co/ maldives-a-paradise-for-tourism-where-christians-are-persecuted/ [accessed 14/07/22].

262 "What does persecution look like in Maldives?", *Open Doors (USA)*, https://www.opendoorsusa.org/christian-persecution/world-watch-list/maldives/ [accessed 14/07/22].

263 "Maldives 2008", *Constitute*, https:// www.constituteproject.org/constitution/ Maldives_2008?lang=en [accessed 14/07/22].

264 ACN, "Maldives", *Religious Freedom in the World Report 2021* https://acninternational.org/ religiousfreedomreport/reports/mv/ [accessed 14/07/22].

265 ACN, "Maldives", *2021*, op. cit.

266 "Maldives", *World Watch List 2022* https://www. opendoorsuk.org/persecution/world-watch-list/ maldives/ [accessed 14/07/22].

267 US State Dept., "Maldives", *2019 Report on International Religious Freedom*, https://www.state.gov/wp-content/ uploads/2020/06/MALDIVES-2019-INTERNATIONAL-RELIGIOUS-FREEDOM-REPORT.pdf [accessed 14/07/22].

268 Ibid.

269 ACN, "Maldives", *2021*, op. cit.

270 "Maldives", World Watch Monitor, https://www. worldwatchmonitor.org/countries/maldives/ [accessed 14/07/22].

271 "Maldives 2008", *Constitute*, op. cit.

272 US State Dept., "Maldives", *2021 Report on International Religious Freedom*, https://www.state.gov/reports/2021-report-on-international-religious-freedom/maldives/ [accessed 14/07/22].

273 Ibid.

274 ACN, "Maldives", *2021*, op. cit.

275 US State Dept., "Maldives", *2021*, op. cit.

276 "Maldives: Extremists behind attack on ex-president", *Alarabiya News*, 8th May 2021 https://english.alarabiya. net/News/world/2021/05/08/Maldives-Extremists-behind-attack-on-ex-president [accessed 14/07/22].

277 US State Dept., "Maldives", *2021*, op. cit.

278 Mohamed Sharuhaan, "Maldives: Islamic extremists behind attack on ex-president", *ABC News*, 8th May 2021 https://abcnews.go.com/International/wireStory/ maldives-islamic-extremists-attack-president-77574167 [accessed 14/07/22].

279 "Islamist extremists attack Yoga Day event in Maldives, President Ibrahim Mohamed Solih orders probe", *Zee News*, 21st June 2022 https://www.msn.com/en-in/ news/newsindia/islamist-extremists-attack-yoga-day-event-in-maldives-president-ibrahim-mohamed-solih-orders-probe/ar-AAYHeQd [accessed 20/07/22].

280 "Maldives: NGO closure shows repression hasn't gone away", *Amnesty International*, 5th November 2019 https://www.amnesty.org/en/latest/news/2019/11/ maldives-ngo-closure-shows-repression-hasnt-gone-away/ [accessed 14/07/22].

281 US State Dept., "Maldives", *2021*, op cit.

282 Ibid.

283 "Maldives: Extremists behind attack on ex-president", *Alarabiya News*, 8th May 2021 https://english.alarabiya. net/News/world/2021/05/08/Maldives-Extremists-behind-attack-on-ex-president [accessed 14/07/22].

284 US State Dept., "Maldives", *2021*, op. cit.

285 Ibid.

286 US State Dept., "Mali", *2021 Report on International Religious Freedom* https://www.state.gov/reports/2021-report-on-international-religious-freedom/mali/ [accessed 01/09/22].

287 ACN, "Mali", *Religious Freedom in the World Report 2021* https://acninternational.org/religiousfreedomreport/ reports/ml/ [accessed 01/09/22].

288 "Mali", *World Watch List 2022* https://media. opendoorsuk.org/document/pdf/2022-Dossiers/ Advocacy-Dossier-Mali.pdf [accessed 01/09/22]; US State Dept., "Mali", *2021,* op. cit.

289 "Mali", *World Watch List,* op. cit.

290 Ibid.

291 Joshua Rhett Miller, "Body of Swiss hostage killed by Al Qaeda affiliate recovered in Mali", *New York Post,* 31st March 2021, https://nypost.com/2021/03/31/body-of-swiss-hostage-killed-by-islamist-group-recovered/ [accessed 25/05/22]; Newton, "Islamist captors beat nun for praying", *ACN (UK) News,* op. cit.

292 US State Dept., "Mali", *2021,* op. cit.

293 Ibid.

294 Ibid.

295 Ibid.

296 "Mali", *World Watch List,* op. cit.

297 US State Dept., "Mali", *2021,* op cit.

298 "Mali", *World Watch List,* op. cit.

299 Ibid.

300 Ibid.

301 US State Dept., "Mali", *2021,* op. cit.

302 Miller, "Body of Swiss hostage…", New York Post, op. cit.

303 "Switzerland says its national hostage in Mali killed", *Al-Jazeera,* 10th October 2020, https://www.aljazeera.com/news/2020/10/10/swiss-hostage-held-in-mali-killed-switzerland [accessed 25/05/22].

304 "Five Abducted Christians in Mali Have Been Freed", *International Christian Concern,* 26th June 2021, https://www.persecution.org/2021/06/26/five-abducted-christians-mali-freed/ [accessed 25/05/22].

305 "Kidnappers free Catholic priest and four others in Mali", *Catholic News Agency,* 24th June 2021, https://www.catholicnewsagency.com/news/248118/kidnappers-free-catholic-priest-and-four-others-in-mali [accessed 25/05/22].

306 Newton, "Islamist captors beat nun…", *ACN (UK) News,* op. cit.

307 John Newton and Maria Lozano, "Jihadists step up terror campaign", *ACN (UK) News,* 3rd December 2021, https://acnuk.org/news/mali-jihadists-steps-up-terror-campaign/ [accessed 25/05/22].

308 "Cabo Ligado Weekly: 20-26 June", *Cabo Ligado,* 28th June 2022 https://acleddata.com/acleddatanew/wp-content/uploads/2022/06/Cabo-Ligado-103.pdf [accessed 14/07/22].

309 "UNHCR Mozambique Cabo Delgado External Update – IDP Response, May 2022", *ReliefWeb,* June 18th 2022 https://reliefweb.int/report/mozambique/unhcr-mozambique-cabo-delgado-external-update-idp-response-may-2022 [accessed 14/07/22].

310 John Newton, "Bishop speaks out following attacks blamed on ISIS", *ACN (UK) News,* April 28th 2020 https://acnuk.org/news/mozambique-bishop-speaks-out-following-attacks-blamed-on-isis/ [accessed 11/07/22].

311 "Mozambique gas project: Total halts work after Palma attacks", *BBC News,* April 26th 2021 https://www.bbc.co.uk/news/world-africa-56886085?msclkid=c956bfd3bb0411ec8b8074fa181756eb [accessed 13/07/22].

312 Fionn Shiner, "Fear and panic as Daesh 'seize' town", *ACN (UK) News,* March 30th 2021 https://acnuk.org/news/mozambique-fear-and-panic-as-daesh-seize-town/ [accessed 11/07/22].

313 Ibid.

314 Ibid.

315 John Newton, Maria Lozano and Paulo Aido, "'How many must die before the world acts?'", *ACN (UK) News,* April 1st 2021 https://acnuk.org/news/mozambique-how-many-more-must-die-before-the-world-acts/ [accessed 12/07/22].

316 Fionn Shiner, "He chose Christ", *ACN (UK) News,* August 12th 2021 https://acnuk.org/news/mozambique-he-chose-christ/ [accessed 11/07/22].

317 *Hear Her Cries,* p. 20.

318 "Winning Peace in Mozambique's Embattled North", *International Crisis Group,* February 10th 2022 https://www.crisisgroup.org/africa/southern-africa/mozambique/b178-winning-peace-mozambiques-embattled-north [accessed 11/07/22].

319 "Islamic State (ISIS) in Mozambique Continues to Attack Christians Villages, Burn Down Homes", *MEMRI,* January 20th 2022 https://www.memri.org/jttm/islamic-state-isis-mozambique-continues-attack-christian-villages-burn-down-homes#_edn1 [accessed 11/07/22].

320 John Newton, "Charity commits fresh help after latest extremists attacks", *ACN (UK) News,* 24th June 2022 https://acnuk.org/news/mozambique-charity-commits-fresh-help-after-latest-extremist-attacks/ [accessed 18/07/22].

321 "You're standing with widow caring for 14 children", *Open Doors (UK),* January 29th 2021 https://www.opendoorsuk.org/news/latest-news/furaia-mozambique/ [accessed 13/04/22].

322 Fionn Shiner, "He chose Christ", *ACN (UK) News,* 12th August 2021 https://acnuk.org/news/mozambique-he-chose-christ/ [accessed 11/07/22].

323 "Islamic State (ISIS) in Mozambique Continues to Attack Christians Villages, Burn Down Homes", *MEMRI,* January 20th 2022 https://www.memri.org/jttm/islamic-state-isis-mozambique-continues-attack-christian-villages-burn-down-homes#_edn1 [accessed 11/07/22].

324 "Spotlight on Global Jihad", *Meir Amit Intelligence and Terrorism Information Center,* 10th March 2022 https://www.terrorism-info.org.il/en/spotlight-on-global-jihad-march-3-9-2022/ [accessed 11/07/22].

325 John Newton, "Charity commits fresh help after latest extremist attacks", *ACN (UK) News,* 24th June 2022 https://acnuk.org/news/mozambique-charity-commits-fresh-help-after-latest-extremist-attacks/ [accessed 18/07/22].

326 Fionn Shiner, Paulo Aido and Maria Lozano, "Nun murdered during deadly attack on church", *ACN (UK) News,* 8th September 2022, https://acnuk.org/news/nun-murdered-during-deadly-attack-on-church/ [accessed 09/09/22].

327 "Nigeria Is Worst in the World for Persecution of Christians in 2021", *Genocide Watch,* 5th April 202[2] https://www.genocidewatch.com/single-post/nigeria-is-worst-in-the-world-for-persecution-of-christians-in-2021 ; "Jihadists Killed 2543 Nigerian Christians in 2022", *Genocide Watch,* 4th July 2022 https://www.genocidewatch.com/single-post/jihadists-have-murdered-2543-nigerian-christians-in-2022 both sites [accessed 19/07/22].

328 Wale Odunsi, "Religious intolerance: 'Boko Haram, ISWAP, bandits killing Christians' – CAN chides US govt", *[Nigeria] Daily Post,* 21st November 2021 https://dailypost.ng/2021/11/21/religious-intolerance-boko-haram-iswap-bandits-killing-christians-can-chides-us-govt/ [accessed 25/05/22].

329 *Hear Her Cries,* p. 26.

330 "Nigeria Is Worst in the World for Persecution of Christians in 2021", *Genocide Watch,* op. cit.

331 Filipe d'Avillez, "Nigerian government has failed Christians", *ACN (Ireland),* [7th June 2022] https://www.acnireland.org/journal/2022/6/7/nigerian-government-has-failed-christians [accessed 21/07/22]; see also Murcadha O Flaherty and John Newton, "Extremists with sophisticated weapons 'kill families, burn houses and destroy crops', says bishop", *ACN (UK) News,* 5th July 2018 https://acnuk.org/news/nigeria-extremists-with-sophisticated-weapons-kill-families-burn-houses-and-destroy-crops-says-archbishop/ [accessed 26/05/22].

332 APPG on international FoRB, *Commentary on the Current state of Freedom of Religion or Belief 2019,* p. 45.

333 "US confirms Boko Haram, bandits working together to blackmail Buhari regime", *Vanguard*, 18th October 2021 https://www.vanguardngr.com/2021/10/us-confirms-boko-haram-bandits-working-together-to-blackmail-buhari-regime/ ; "Kidnapping: ISWAP, Boko Haram training bandits, says NIS", *Punch*, 7th August 2001 https://punchng.com/kidnapping-iswap-boko-haram-training-bandits-says-nis/ ; "Gunmen Kill 34 in New Attack in Northwest Nigeria", *Defense Post*, 23rd March 2022 https://www.thedefensepost.com/2022/03/23/gunmen-attack-northwest-nigeria/ [all sites accessed 16/05/22].

334 "Nigeria Is Worst in the World for Persecution of Christians in 2021", *Genocide Watch*, 5th April 2021 https://www.genocidewatch.com/single-post/nigeria-is-worst-in-the-world-for-persecution-of-christians-in-2021 ; "470 Killed, 820 Disappeared And 3,250 Abducted In Eastern Nigeria By Security Forces In 220 Days (Jan-10th August 2021)", *Intersociety*, [nd 2021] https://intersociety-ng.org/470-killed-820-disappeared-and-3250-abducted-in-eastern-nigeria-by-security-forces-in-220-days-jan-10th-august-2021/ [both sites accessed 26/05/22].

335 "Professor Tarfa released on bail", CSW, 10th December 2020.

336 John Pontifex, "The Rosary inspired my captors to release me", *ACN (UK) News*, 17th December 2020 https://acnuk.org/news/nigeria-the-rosary-inspired-my-captors-to-release-me/ [accessed 19/05/22].

337 Fionn Shiner, "Catholic priest murdered" *ACN (UK) News*, 18th January 2021 https://acnuk.org/news/nigeria-catholic-priest-murdered/ [accessed 19/05/22].

338 Tim Wyatt "Nigerian girl escapes Boko Haram, seven years after her kidnap", *Church Times*, 19th February 2021 https://www.churchtimes.co.uk/articles/2021/19-february/news/world/nigerian-girl-escapes-boko-haram-seven-years-after-her-kidnap [accessed 25/05/22].

339 "Four Women abducted as Kaduna State kidnaping crisis continues", CSW, 26th April 2021.

340 "Many Killed, Others Kidnapped as Bandits Attack Churches in Kaduna", *Sahara Reporters*, 5th May 2021 http://saharareporters.com/2021/05/05/breaking-many-killed-others-kidnapped-bandits-attack-churches-kaduna [accessed 19/05/22].

341 "Attackers kidnap 140 pupils from Nigerian boarding school", *Guardian*, 5th July 2021 https://www.theguardian.com/world/2021/jul/05/attackers-kidnap-pupils-from-nigerian-boarding-school-bethel-baptist-kaduna [accessed 19/05/22].

342 "ISWAP Terrorists Now Block Maiduguri-Damaturu Road, Abduct Christian Passengers, Leave Muslims — Borno Cleric", *Sahara Reporters*, 23rd July 2021 http://saharareporters.com/2021/07/23/iswap-terrorists-now-block-maiduguri-damaturu-road-abduct-christian-passengers-leave [accessed 25/05/22].

343 *Hear Her Cries*, p. 29.

344 Steven Kefas, "Bloody Sunday in Southern Kaduna as Terrorist Herdsmen Kill 30, Burn Several Houses", *Middle Belt Times*, 27th September 2021 https://middlebelttimes.com/2021/09/27/breaking-bloody-sunday-in-southern-kaduna-as-terrorist-herdsmen-kill-30-burn-several-houses [accessed 26/05/22]; "Attack on Christians in Nigeria described as a 'massacre'", *CNA*, 30th September 2021 https://www.catholicnewsagency.com/news/249138/attack-on-christians-in-nigeria-described-as-a-massacre both sites [accessed 26/05/22].

345 John Pontifex, "Three seminarians abducted from chapel", *ACN (UK) News*, 12th October 2021 https://acnuk.org/news/nigeria-three-seminarians-abducted-from-chapel/ ; Filipe D'Avillez and John Pontifex, "Kidnapped seminarians released", *ACN (UK) News:* 14th October 2021 https://acnuk.org/news/nigeria-kidnapped-seminarians-released/ both sites [accessed 19/05/22].

346 "ISWAP Terrorists Kill 12 Christians in Borno State, Nigeria", *Morning Star News*, 21st December 2021 https://morningstarnews.org/2021/12/iswap-terrorists-kill-12-christians-in-borno-state-nigeria/ [accessed 25/05/22].

347 Ibrahim Hassan-Wuyo, "SHOCKER! Kidnapped Bethel student refuses to return, says he's comfortable with bandits", *Vanguard*, 6th February 2022 https://www.vanguardngr.com/2022/02/shocker-kidnapped-bethel-student-refuses-to-return-says-hes-comfortable-with-bandits/ [accessed 27/05/22].

348 "Terrorists Kill 50 Christians and Abduct 100, including Priest", *Morning Star News*, 28th March 2022 https://morningstarnews.org/2022/03/terrorists-kill-50-christians-and-abduct-100-including-priest [accessed 14/04/22].

349 Fionn Shiner, "Was kidnapped priest tortured to death?", *ACN (UK) News*, 29th April 2022 https://acnuk.org/news/nigeria-was-kidnapped-priest-tortured-to-death/ ; Fionn Shiner "Kidnapped priest killed as another is abducted", *ACN (UK) News*, 12th May 2022 https://acnuk.org/news/nigeria-kidnapped-priest-killed-as-another-is-abducted/ both sites [accessed 18/05/22].

350 Maria Lozano, "Student stoned and burned to death", *ACN (UK) News*, 13th May 2022 https://acnuk.org/news/nigeria-student-stoned-and-burned-to-death/ ; John Newton "New suspects sought for murder of Christian girl in Nigeria", *ACN (UK) News*, 18th May 2022 https://acnuk.org/news/nigeria-new-suspects-sought-for-murder-of-christian-girl-in-nigeria/ [both sites accessed 18/05/22].

351 "Newly Released ISIS Video Depicts Execution of Nigerian Christians", *International Christian Concern*, 19th May 2022 https://www.persecution.org/2022/05/19/newly-released-isis-video-depicts-execution-nigerian-christians/ [accessed 25/05/22].

352 John Newton, "50 killed during Pentecost Sunday massacre at Catholic church", *ACN (UK) News*, 6th June 2022 https://acnuk.org/news/nigeria-50-killed-during-pentecost-sunday-massacre-at-catholic-church/ [accessed 07/06/22].

353 "Over 32 Villagers Killed After Helicopter Helped Killer Herders Burn Down Southern Kaduna Community, Says Local Group", *Sahara Reporters*, 8th June 2022 https://saharareporters.com/2022/06/08/over-32-villagers-killed-after-helicopter-helped-killer-herders-burn-down-southern-kaduna ; "Survivors Of Gunmen Attack Aided By 'Strange Helicopter' In Kaduna State Narrate Bitter Ordeals", *Sahara Reporters*, 13th June 2022 https://saharareporters.com/2022/06/13/survivors-gunmen-attack-aided-strange-helicopter-kaduna-state-narrate-bitter-ordeals [both sites accessed 16/06/22].

354 "Two Weeks After Ondo Terrorist Attack, Gunmen Storm Catholic Church In Kaduna, Kill Three Worshippers, Abduct Many", *Sahara Reporters*, 19th June 2022 https://saharareporters.com/2022/06/19/breaking-two-weeks-after-ondo-terrorist-attack-gunmen-storm-catholic-church-kaduna-kill ; "Suspected Terrorists Attack Four Kaduna Communities, Kidnap 36 Residents" *Sahara Reporters*, 20th June 2022 http://saharareporters.com/2022/06/20/suspected-terrorists-attack-four-kaduna-communities-kidnap-36-residents [both sites accessed 21/06/22].

355 "Christian Killed, Church Leader Kidnapped in Nigeria", *Morning Star News*, 13th September https://morningstarnews.org/2022/09/christian-killed-church-leader-kidnapped-in-nigeria/ [accessed 14/09/22].

356 US State Dept., "North Korea", *2021 Report on International Religious Freedom* https://www.state.gov/reports/2021-report-on-international-religious-freedom/north-korea/ [accessed 15/07/22].

357 Fyodor Tertitskiy, "How the North is run: the secret police", *NK PRO*, 24th July 2018 https://www.nknews.org/pro/how-the-north-is-run-the-secret-police-2/ [accessed 15/07/22].

358 US State Dept. "North Korea", *2020 Report on International Religious Freedom* https://www.state.

gov/reports/2020-report-on-international-religious-freedom/north-korea/ [accessed 15/07/22].

359 US State Dept., "North Korea", 2021, op. cit.

360 Marcus Holland, "Religious Persecution in North Korea", Peterson Institute for International Economics, 30th September 2016 https://www.piie.com/blogs/north-korea-witness-transformation/religious-persecution-north-korea [accessed 15/07/22].

361 US State Dept., "North Korea", 2022 Annual Report, p.26 https://www.uscirf.gov/sites/default/files/2022-06/2022%20USCIRF%20Annual%20Report.pdf [accessed 15/07/22].

362 Ibid., p.26

363 Olivia Cavallaro, "North Korea intensifies Christian persecution by portraying them as 'Blood-Sucking Monsters'," Christianity Daily, 24th September 2021 https://www.christianitydaily.com/articles/13379/20210924/north-korea-intensifies-christian-persecution-by-portraying-them-as-blood-sucking-monsters.htm [accessed 15/07/22].

364 "Inquiry into Human Rights Violations in North Korea 2014-2020/1", All-Party Parliamentary Group on North Korea, July 2021, p.4 https://www.appgnorthkoreainquiry.com/_files/ugd/897883_774041 7d3bb04474807a9e9679d6b2ec.pdf [accessed 15/07/22].

365 Ibid., p.4.

366 "Persecuting Faith: Documenting religious freedom violations in North Korea (Volume 2), KoreaFuture, 2021, p.52. https://static1.squarespace.com/static/608ae0498089c163350e0ff5/t/6185747b98a32923 b43b7de8/1636136111825/Persecuting+Faith+-+Documenting+religious+freedom+violations+in+North+Korea+%28Volume+2%29.pd [accessed 15/07/22].

367 US State Dept., "North Korea", 2022, op. cit, p. 26.

368 US State Dept., "North Korea", 2020, op. cit.

369 Olivia Cavallaro, "North Korea intensifies Christian persecution…", op. cit.

370 "Launching a new database and report on religious freedom", KoreaFuture, 28th October 2021 https://www.koreafuture.org/news/religious-freedom-28xp2 [accessed 15/07/22].

371 US State Dept. "North Korea", 2020, op. cit.

372 "Inquiry into Human Rights Violations in North Korea 2014-2020/1", All-Party Parliamentary Group on North Korea, July 2021, p.4 https://www.appgnorthkoreainquiry.com/_files/ugd/897883_774041 7d3bb04474807a9e9679d6b2ec.pdf [accessed 15/07/22].

373 US State Dept., "North Korea", 2021, op. cit.

374 "Life as a Persecuted Christian", Missions Box, 3rd February 2022 https://missionsbox.org/news/life-persecuted-christian-north-korea-baes-story/ [accessed 15/07/22].

375 "Martyrs of Pyongyang and the war: the diocesan investigation for beatification ends", Asianews, 9th June 2022 https://www.Asianews.it/news-en/Martyrs-of-Pyongyang-and-the-war:-the-diocesan-investigation-for-beatification-ends-55999.html [accessed 15/07/22].

376 John Pontifex, "Taliban threat – Churches increase security", ACN (UK) News, 2nd September 2021 https://acnuk.org/news/pakistan-taliban-thr https://acnuk.org/news/pakistan-taliban-threat-churches-increase-security/eat-churches-increase-security/ [accessed 14/07/22].

377 USCIRF, "Pakistan", 2022 Annual Report, p. 28 https://www.uscirf.gov/sites/default/files/2022-04/2022 USCIRF Annual Report_1.pdf [accessed 30/06/22].

378 US State Dept., "Pakistan", 2021 Report on International Religious Freedom https://www.state.gov/reports/2021-report-on-international-religious-freedom/pakistan/ [accessed 14/07/22].

379 "Maira Shahbaz: the story so far", https://acnuk.org/maira-shahbaz-petition-page/ [accessed 14/07/22].

380 Lydia Catling, "Christian nurse is 'tied up and tortured by mob at Pakistani hospital after Muslim colleague falsely accused her of blasphemy'", Daily Mail, 1st February 2021 https://www.dailymail.co.uk/news/article-9211481/Christian-nurse-tortured-mob-Pakistani-hospital-colleague-falsely-accused-blasphemy.html [accessed 14/07/22].

381 John Newton, "Archbishop's plea for abducted and abused minors", ACN (UK) News, 13th July 2022 https://acnuk.org/news/pakistan-archbishops-fresh-please-for-abducted-and-abused-minors/ [accessed 13/07/22].

382 Hear Her Cries, pp. 30 ff.

383 Bob Smietana, "Forced conversions, marriages spike in Pakistan", RNS, 6th June 2019 https://religionnews.com/2019/06/06/forced-conversions-marriages-spike-in-pakistan/ [accessed 14/07/22].

384 "Preamble – The Constitution of Pakistan, Pakistani.org https://www.pakistani.org/pakistan/constitution/preamble.html [accessed 14/07/22].

385 US State Dept., "Pakistan", 2021, op cit

386 USCIRF, "Pakistan", 2022, op. cit.

387 "Christians want demolition notices withdrawn", DAWN, 1st September 2020 https://www.dawn.com/news/1580741 [accessed 14/07/22].

388 "Pakistan: Assessment- 2022", South Asia Terrorism https://www.satp.org/terrorism-assessment/pakistan# [accessed 14/07/22].

389 Kaleem Dean, "The myth of equal rights: religious minorities in Pakistan", Daily Times, 23rd March 2017 https://dailytimes.com.pk/21623/the-myth-of-equal-rights-religious-minorities-in-pakistan/ [accessed 14/07/22].

390 "Pakistan SC asks Imran Khan govt about 30,000 vacant jobs", Malaysia Sun, 29th September 2021 https://www.malaysiasun.com/news/271337784/pakistan-sc-asks-imran-khan-govt-about-30000-vacant-jobs [accessed 14/07/22].

391 Marweati, "Blasphemy Laws in Pakistan and the Influx of Refugees", international refugee law, 12th May 2013 https://internationalrefugeelaw.wordpress.com/2013/05/12/blasphemy-laws-in-pakistan-and-the-influx-of-refugees [accessed 14/07/22].

392 "Guilty until proven innocent: The sacrilegious nature of blasphemy laws in Pakistan", European Foundation for South Asian Studies, April 2020 https://www.efsas.org/publications/study-papers/guilty-until-proven-innocent-the-sacrilegious-nature-of-blasphemy-laws-in-pakistan/ [accessed 14/07/22].

393 USCIRF, "Pakistan", 2022, op cit.

394 Muhammad Shahzad, "42 Muslims accused of blasphemy in 2021", Express Tribune, 8th March 2022 https://tribune.com.pk/story/2346951/42-muslims-accused-of-blasphemy-in-2021 [accessed 14/07/22].

395 Kamran Chaudhry, "Punjab passes bill to protect Islam", Union of Catholic Asian News, 23rd July 2020 https://www.UCANews.com/news/punjab-passes-bill-to-protect-islam/88885# [accessed 14/07/22].

396 "From Our Member National Commission for Justice and Peace (NCJP), Pakistan – Education & Religious Freedom: a fact sheet", Asian Forum for Human Rights and Development, 1st August 2019 https://www.forum-asia.org/?p=29457 [accessed 14/07/22].

397 "Pakistan: Christian woman denounced for blasphemy", Independent Catholic News, 31st July 2021 https://www.indcatholicnews.com/news/41447 [accessed 14/07/22].

398 John Pontifex, "Our little angel is back home", ACN (UK) News, 17th February 2021 https://acnuk.org/news/pakistan-our-little-angel-is-back-home/ [accessed 14/07/22].

399 Shafique Khokhar, "Muslim mob attacks a Christian village. Houses looted, men and women beaten and injured (VIDEO)", Asianews, 18th May 2021 https://www.Asianews.it/news-en/Muslim-mob-attacks-a-Christian-village.-Houses-looted,-men-and-women-beaten-and-injured-(VIDEO)-53169.html [accessed 14/07/22].

400 Ishaq Tanoli, "Underage marriage: SHC allows Arzoo to leave shelter home, return to her parents", DAWN, 22nd

December 2021 https://www.dawn.com/news/1665223 [accessed 14/07/22].

401 Shafique Khokhar, "Christian cleaner of Koran publisher jailed for blasphemy", *Asianews,* 14th June 2022 https://www.Asianews.it/news-en/Christian-cleaner-of-Koran-publisher-jailed-for-blasphemy-56027.html [accessed 14/07/22].

402 John Pontifex, "Tributes to Christian man killed in Peshawar", *ACN (UK) News,* 31st January 2022 https://acnuk.org/news/pakistan-tributes-to-christian-man-killed-in-peshawar/ [accessed 14/07/22].

403 Fionn Shiner, "I was tortured, threatened with rape and death – but I'll never deny Jesus", *ACN (UK) News,* 5th May 2022 https://acnuk.org/news/pakistan-i-was-tortured-threatened-with-rape-and-death-but-ill-never-deny-jesus/ [accessed 14/07/22].

404 "Maira Shahbaz – religious prisoners of conscience", *USCIRF* https://www.uscirf.gov/religious-prisoners-conscience/forb-victims-database/maira-shahbaz [accessed 14/07/22].

405 "Maira's refuge? Apostasy, asylum and religious freedom", *The Article,* 1st August 2021 https://www.thearticle.com/mairas-refuge-apostasy-asylum-and-religious-freedom [accessed 14/07/22].

406 "Christian Man hacked by sickles then tied around neck with hose and dragged through streets to nearby home", *British Asian Christian Association,* 23rd June 2022, https://archive.aweber.com/newsletter/awlist6137597/MTQ5MTQzMTg=/christian-man-hacked-by-sickles-then-tied-around-neck-with-hose-and-dragged-through-streets-to-nearby-home.htm [accessed 16/09/22].

407 John Newton, "Archbishop's fresh plea for abducted and abused minors", *ACN (UK) News,* 13th July 2022 https://acnuk.org/news/pakistan-archbishops-fresh-please-for-abducted-and-abused-minors/ [accessed 14/07/22].

408 "Christian woman raped by employer then gang tells her and family they must go back to work", *British Asian Christian Association,* 17th July 2022 https://www.britishasianchristians.org/baca-news/christian-woman-raped/ [accessed 10/08/22].

409 "A Christian sentenced to death on false accusations of blasphemy", *Fides,* 26th July 2022 http://www.fides.org/en/news/72581-ASIA_PAKISTAN_A_Christian_sentenced_to_death_on_false_accusations_of_blasphemy ; Kevin Zeller, "Pakistani Christian mechanic sentenced to death for blasphemy", *Mission Network News,* 15th July https://www.mnnonline.org/news/pakistani-christian-mechanic-sentenced-to-death-for-blasphemy/ [both sites accessed 11/08/22].

410 "One killed in shooting at Christian colony in Pakistan", *UCANews,* 9th August 2022, https://www.ucanews.com/news/one-killed-in-shooting-at-christian-colony-in-pakistan/98344 [accessed 16/09/22].

411 John Newton and Maria Lozano, "ACN helps women stand up to prejudice and discrimination", *ACN (UK) News,* 25th June 2021 https://acnuk.org/news/pakistan-acn-helps-women-stand-up-to-prejudice-and-discrimination/ [accessed 25/07/22].

412 "Qatar", *Constitute,* https://www.constituteproject.org/constitution/Qatar_2003?lang=en [accessed 29/06/22].

413 US State Dept., "Qatar", *2021 Report on International Religious Freedom,* https://www.state.gov/reports/2021-report-on-international-religious-freedom/qatar/ ; "Christianity in Qatar", *Harvard Divinity School,* https://rpl.hds.harvard.edu/faq/christianity-qatar [both sites accessed 29/06/22].

414 "Church Grows in Qatar Despite Challenges", *International Christian Concern,* 10th October 2019 https://www.persecution.org/2019/01/10/church-grows-qatar-despite-challenges/ [accessed 29/06/22].

415 "Christianity in Qatar", *Harvard Divinity School,* op. cit.

416 US State Dept., "Qatar", *2021,* op. cit.

417 "How many Christians are there in Qatar", *Open Doors,* https://www.opendoorsuk.org/persecution/world-watch-list/qatar/ [accessed 29/06/22].

418 US State Dept., "Qatar", 2021, op. cit.

419 "Saudi Arabia Revises Radical Textbooks", *International Christian Concern,* 2nd January 2021 https://www.persecution.org/2021/02/01/saudi-arabia-revises-radical-textbooks/ [accessed 30/06/22].

420 "Qatar: Extremism and Terrorism", *Counter Extremism Project,* https://www.counterextremism.com/countries/qatar-extremism-and-terrorism [accessed 29/06/22].

421 Ibid.

422 Eldad J Pardo, "Understanding Qatari Ambition: The Curriculum 2016-20 (Interim Report)", p.1, IMPACT-sehttps://www.impact-se.org/wp-content/uploads/Understanding-Qatari-Ambition_The-Curriculum-2016-20.pdf [accessed 29/06/22]; "Saudi Arabia Revises Radical Textbooks", *International Christian Concern,* op. cit.

423 US State Dept., "Qatar", *2021,* op. cit.

424 Ibid.

425 "Qatar-based charity organizations a façade, fuel global terrorism: Report", *The Print,* 11th June 2022 https://theprint.in/world/qatar-based-charity-organizations-a-facade-fuel-global-terrorism-report/992228/ [accessed 29/06/22].

426 USCIRF, "Russia", *2022 Annual Report* https://www.uscirf.gov/sites/default/files/2022-04/2022%20Russia.pdf [accessed 20/06/22].

427 "Q&A: breaches of international law and human rights issues", *Norwegian Helsinki Committee,* 20th March 2014 http://www.nhc.no/en/qa-breaches-of-international-law-and-human-rights-issues-2/ ; Freedom House, "Crimea", *Freedom in the World 2020* https://freedomhouse.org/country/crimea/freedom-world/2020 [both sites accessed 20/06/22].

428 APPG for International FoRB, *Commentary on the current state of Freedom of Religion or Belief 2020,* p. 51.

429 "Court orders parish to destroy its chapel", *Forum 18,* 9th December 2019 http://www.forum18.org/archive.php?article_id=2526 ; Halya Coynash, "Russia moves to crush Orthodox Church of Ukraine in occupied Crimea", *Kharkiv Human Rights Protection Group,* 14th February 2019 https://khpg.org/en/1550095831 [both sites accessed 01/06/22].

430 Felix Corley, "23 fines under Russia's 'anti-missionary' laws in 2021", *Forum 18,* 22nd February 2022 https://www.forum18.org/archive.php?article_id=2720 [accessed 14/04/22].

431 "Russia Tightens Restrictions on Churches and Missionary Activity", *International Christian Concern,* 5th April 2021 https://www.persecution.org/2021/06/01/russia-tightens-restrictions-churches-missionary-activity/ [accessed 01/06/22].

432 "Activity of Religious Group of Baptists forbidden in Anapa", *Kuban24,* 20th February 2021; "Baptists in Anapa forbidden a second time to engage in Evangelism", *Argumenty i fakty,* 20th February 2021; "Baptists forbidden to work in Anapa until removal of violations", *Interfax-Religii,* 20th February 2021 via Russia Religion News https://www2.stetson.edu/religious-news/210220a.html [accessed 31/05/22].

433 "Adygea Pastors accused of illegal evangelism", *Kavkaz Realii,* 24th June 2021 via Russia Religion News https://www2.stetson.edu/religious-news/210624h.html [accessed 31/05/22].

434 "Leader of Religious Group attracts prosecutor's attention in Novosergievka District", *Orenday,* 17th March

2021 via Russia Religion News https://www2.stetson.edu/religious-news/210317a.html [accessed 31/05/22].

435 "E.Kh.B. minister fined for 'illegal' Evangelism in Obninsk", *SOVA Center for News and Analysis*, 23ʳᵈ April 2021 via Russia Religion News https://www2.stetson.edu/religious-news/210423b.html [accessed 31/05/22].

436 "'Bread of Life' Church of Christians of Evangelical Faith in Kerch fined 30,000 rubles", *Article 28*, 31ˢᵗ May 2021 via *Russia Religion News* https://www2.stetson.edu/religious-news/210531a.html [accessed 31/05/22].

437 Felix Corley, "23 fines under Russia's 'anti-missionary' laws in 2021", *Forum 18*, 22ⁿᵈ February 2022 https://www.forum18.org/archive.php?article_id=2720 [accessed 14/04/22].

438 "In Samara, Church building being dismantled fell onto neighboring house", *Tsargrad.tv*, 4ᵗʰ September 2021; "It piled up on the roof of house next door: Consequences of collapse of wall of Church in Samara", *63.ru*, 6ᵗʰ September 2021; "In Samara, demolition of Catholic Church in Mekhzavod begins", *Domostroyrf.ru*, 31ˢᵗ August 2021 trans. Russia Religion News https://www2.stetson.edu/religious-news/210904a.html [accessed 31/05/22].

439 Victoria Arnold, "Patriarchate priest fined for condemning war in Ukraine", *Forum 18*, 11ᵗʰ March 2022 https://www.forum18.org/archive.php?article_id=2725 [accessed 01/06/22].

440 "Аксенов поручил разработать проект о национализации имущества украинских олигархов в РФ", *Tass*, 30ᵗʰ March 2022 https://tass.ru/politika/14229709 [accessed 31/03/22].

441 Victoria Arnold, "Second Orthodox priest facing criminal charges for opposing Ukraine war", *Forum 18*, 11ᵗʰ July https://www.forum18.org/archive.php?article_id=2757 [accessed 15/07/22].

442 "Welcome to The Apostolic Vicariate of Northern Arabia", http://www.avona.org/saudi/saudi_about.htm#.W0kGSNJKjIU [accessed 30/06/22].

443 Carey Lodge, "Muslims converting to Christianity in Saudi Arabia, despite intense persecution", *Christian Today*, 31ˢᵗ May 2016 https://www.christiantoday.com/article/muslims-converting-to-christianity-in-saudi-arabia-despite-intense-persecution/87220.htm [accessed 30/06/22].

444 US State Dept., "Saudi Arabia", *2019 Report on International Religious Freedom*, https://www.state.gov/reports/2019-report-on-international-religious-freedom/saudi-arabia/ [accessed 30/06/22].

445 "Saudi Arabia – Constitution: Adopted by Royal Decree of King Fahd – March 1992", *Saudi Network* http://www.the-saudi.net/saudi-arabia/saudi-constitution.htm [accessed 27/07/22].

446 US State Dept., "Saudi Arabia", *2019*, op. cit.

447 Ibid.

448 US State Dept., "Saudi Arabia", *2020 Report on International Religious Freedom* https://www.state.gov/reports/2020-report-on-international-religious-freedom/saudi-arabia/ [accessed 30/06/22].

449 USCIRF, "Saudi Arabia", *2022 Annual Report*, p.32 https://www.uscirf.gov/sites/default/files/2022-04/2022%20Saudi%20Arabia.pdf [accessed 30/06/22].

450 US State Dept., "Saudi Arabia", *2020*, op. cit.

451 Eldad J. Pardo, *Review of Selected Saudi Textbooks 2020–21* (Ramat Gan: Impact-Se, 2020/21) https://www.impact-se.org/wp-content/uploads/Review-of-Selected-Saudi-Textbooks-2020-21.pdf [accessed 09/08/22].

452 "Saudi mufti tells young Saudis not to heed call to jihad," *Reuters*, 28ᵗʰ August 2014 http://www.reuters.com/article/us-saudi-security-idUSKBN0GS19M20140828 [accessed 30/06/22].

453 Rayhan Uddin, "Mecca sermon raises questions on possible Saudi normalisaton with Israel", *Middle East Eye*, 6ᵗʰ September 2020 https://www.middleeasteye.net/news/saudi-israel-normalisation-mecca-sermon-sudais [accessed 30/05/22].

454 "Islamic State claims responsibility for Jeddah attack", *Wantra.de*, 13ᵗʰ November 2020 https://en.qantara.de/content/islamic-state-claims-responsibility-for-jeddah-attack [accessed 30/06/22].

455 US State Dept., "Saudi Arabia", *2021 Report on International Religious Freedom*, https://www.state.gov/reports/2021-report-on-international-religious-freedom/saudi-arabia/ [accessed 30/06/22].

456 "Saudi Arabia Revises Radical Textbooks", *International Christian Concern*, 2ⁿᵈ January 2021 https://www.persecution.org/2021/02/01/saudi-arabia-revises-radical-textbooks/ [accessed 30/06/22].

457 "World faith leaders convene in Saudi Arabia for first time", *ETN*, 13ᵗʰ May, https://eturbonews.com/world-faith-leaders-convene-in-saudi-arabia-for-first-time/ [accessed 30/06/22].

458 "Queen Elizabeth II: Saudi police arrest man after dedicating Umrah pilgrimage to late monarch", *Middle East Eye*, 13ᵗʰ September 2022, https://www.middleeasteye.net/news/queen-elizabeth-saudi-arabia-arrests-man-dedicating-pilgrimage [accessed 15/09/22].

459 "Saudi Arabia arrests man over pilgrimage for Queen Elizabeth", *AP News*, 13ᵗʰ September 2022, https://apnews.com/article/entertainment-middle-east-religion-arrests-1b58678cf913c75f564fdb48e9f9db99 [accessed 15/09/22].

460 *Prejudice and Patronage: An Analysis of Incidents of Violence against Christians, Muslims, and Hindus in Sri Lanka (September 2019 – September 2020)* (Colombo: Verité Research, 2021), p. 9 https://www.veriteresearch.org/wp-content/uploads/2021/06/VR_Eng_RR_Mar2021_Prejudice-and-Patronage-An-Analysis-of-Incidents-of-Violence-against-Christians-Muslims-and-Hindus-in-Sri-Lanka.pdf [accessed 06/05/22].

461 Rebecca Paveley, "Minority religious groups under attack in Sri Lanka, says Church of Ceylon", *Church Times*, 8ᵗʰ October 2021 https://www.churchtimes.co.uk/articles/2021/8-october/news/world/minority-religious-groups-under-attack-in-sri-lanka-says-church-of-ceylon [accessed 06/05/22].

462 John Newton, "'Why did 269 people die?': Cardinal slams authorities for lack of answers – suggests collusion", *ACN (UK) News*, 21ˢᵗ March 2022 https://acnuk.org/news/sri-lanka-why-did-269-people-die/ [accessed 06/05/22].

463 Melani Manel Perera, "Sri Lankan Christians criticise Mahinda Rajapaksa's hypocrisy", *Asianews*, 13ᵗʰ September 2021 https://www.Asianews.it/news-en/Sri-Lankan-Christians-criticise-Mahinda-Rajapaksa%27s-hypocrisy-54047.html [accessed 06/05/22].

464 "Pastor Ordered to Stop Worship Activities", *Voice of the Martyrs (Canada)*, 19ᵗʰ November 2020 https://www.vomcanada.com/lk-2020-11-19.htm 04/04/22.

465 "Sri Lanka urged to end mandatory cremation of Covid victims", *UCA News*, 5ᵗʰ January 2021 (updated version) https://www.UCA News.com/news/sri-lanka-urged-to-end-mandatory-cremation-of-covid-victims/90872 [accessed 23/03/22]; "Sri Lanka: Compulsory Cremation Divides Society", *SSPX News*, 27ᵗʰ January 2022 https://fsspx.news/en/news-events/news/sri-lanka-compulsory-cremation-divides-society-63576 [accessed 29/03/22].

466 "Churches Face Threats and Questioning", *Voice of the Martyrs (Canada)*, 15ᵗʰ April 2021 https://www.vomcanada.com/lk-2021-04-15.htm [accessed 04/04/22].

467 "Family Refused Christian Burial", *Voice of the Martyrs (Canada)*, 14th October 2021 https://www.vomcanada.com/lk-2021-10-14.htm [accessed 04/04/22].

468 Meera Srinivasan, "Hardline monk to head legal reforms panel in Sri Lanka", *The Hindu*, 27th October 2021 https://www.thehindu.com/news/international/sri-lankan-president-appoints-task-force-led-by-controversial-buddhist-monk-for-one-country-one-law/article37189262.ece ; "Sri Lankan Church opposes government's 'one country, one law' plan", *Vatican News*, 4th November 2021 https://www.vaticannews.va/en/church/news/2021-11/sri-lanka-bishops-oppose-government-one-law-one-law-plan.html ; "Sri Lanka president extends tenure of controversial 'One Country, One Law' task force", *Economy Next*, 1st March 2022 https://economynext.com/sri-lanka-president-extends-tenure-of-controversial-one-country-one-law-task-force-91025/ [all sites accessed 06/05/22].

469 "Christians Beaten Following Prayer Meeting", *Voice of the Martyrs (Canada)*, 16th December 2021 https://www.vomcanada.com/lk-2021-12-16.htm 04/04/22.

470 "Mob Demanded Christians to Stop Worship", *Voice of the Martyrs (Canada)*, 17th March 2022 https://www.vomcanada.com/lk-2022-03-17.htm [accessed 04/04/22].

471 "Omas al-Bashir ousted: How Sudan got here", BBC News, 11th April 2019 https://www.bbc.co.uk/news/world-africa-47892742 [accessed 04/05/22].

472 Stoyan Zaimov, "Sudan's President, who has persecuted Christians 'Under Shariah Law,' is on the run after UN calls for his arrest for War Crimes", *Christian Post*, 15th June 2015, https://www.christianpost.com/news/sudans-president-who-has-persecuted-christians-under-shariah-law-is-on-the-run-after-un-calls-for-his-arrest-for-war-crimes.html [accessed 04/05/22].

473 "Changes in criminal law as Sudan annuls apostasy death sentence", *Al-Jazeera*, 12th July 2020 https://www.aljazeera.com/news/2020/7/12/changes-in-criminal-law-as-sudan-annuls-apostasy-death-sentence [accessed 04/05/22].

474 Ibid.

475 Ibid.

476 US State Dept., "Sudan", *2020 Report on International Religious Freedom* https://www.state.gov/reports/2020-report-on-international-religious-freedom/sudan/ [accessed 24/05/22].

477 Ivana Kottasová and Eliza Mackintosh, "The military has taken over in Sudan. Here's what happened", *CCN*, 26th October 2021 https://edition.cnn.com/2021/10/25/africa/sudan-coup-explained-intl-cmd/index.html [accessed 04/05/22].

478 "Interference in Church affairs continues under military rule", *CSW*, 14th January 2022 https://www.csw.org.uk/2022/01/14/press/5548/article.htm [accessed 25/07/22].

479 Lindy Lowry, "Sudan Christin calls for urgent prayer as military seizes power", *Open Doors (USA)*, 26th October 2021 https://www.opendoorsusa.org/christian-persecution/stories/breaking-sudan-christian-calls-for-urgent-prayer-as-military-seizes-power/ [accessed 04/05/22].

480 "Pressure Sudan's Military to Value Human Life: Catholic Bishop to International Community", *ACI Africa*, 25th October 2021 https://www.aciafrica.org/news/4548/pressure-sudans-military-to-value-human-life-catholic-bishop-to-international-community [accessed 04/05/22].

481 "Primate of South Sudan urges prayer for Bishop of Abyei after 'barbaric attack' at Dungob Alei", *Anglican Communion News Service*, May 18th 2021 https://www.anglicannews.org/news/2021/05/primate-of-south-sudan-urges-prayer-for-bishop-of-abyei-after-barbaric-attack-at-dungob-alei.aspx [accessed 02/04/22].

482 Ibid.

483 Ibid.

484 "Sudanese Church of Christ building burned down in Tamboul", *CSW*, 8th January 2021 https://www.csw.org.uk/2021/01/08/press/4938/article.htm [accessed 04/05/22].

485 Agnes Aineah, "Advocate for Christians attacked in Sudan", *Catholic News Agency*, 7th July 2021 https://www.catholicnewsagency.com/news/248294/advocate-for-christians-attacked-in-sudan [accessed 03/05/22].

486 "Church Building Locked, Leaders Arrested in Sudan", *Morning Star News*, 6th March 2022 https://morningstarnews.org/2022/03/church-building-locked-leaders-arrested-in-sudan/ [accessed 03/05/22].

487 "Attacked Pastor in Sudan, Elder Sentences to Month in Jail", *Morning Star News*, 25th April 2022 https://christiannews.net/2022/04/25/attacked-pastor-in-sudan-elder-sentenced-to-month-in-jail/ [accessed 03/05/22].

488 "Christian Couple in Sudan Faces Possible Flogging for 'Adultery'", *Morning Star News*, 3rd May 2022 https://christiannews.net/2022/05/03/christian-couple-in-sudan-faces-possible-flogging-for-adultery/ [accessed 03/05/22].

489 "Evangelical church properties threatened with demolition", *CSW*, 25th May 2022 https://www.csw.org.uk/2022/05/25/press/5717/article.htm [accessed 25/07/22].

490 "Four men charged with apostasy", *CSW*, 8th July 2022 https://www.csw.org.uk/2022/07/08/press/5766/article.htm [accessed 12/07/22].

491 "Syria: after decade of War, Christian population collapses", *Ansa Med*, 18th August 2021 https://www.ansamed.info/ansamed/en/news/sections/generalnews/2021/08/18/syria-after-decade-of-war-christian-population-collapses_8d169081-4d73-4719-af02-909e91387f3d.html ; USCIRF, "Syria", *2022 Annual Report*, p.35 https://www.uscirf.gov/sites/default/files/2022-04/2022 USCIRF Annual Report_1.pdf [both sites accessed 27/06/22].

492 "Many Christians are short of hope, but any they do find comes from the Church", *ACN (International)*, 30th March 2022 https://acninternational.org/interview-to-regina-lynch-after-the-catholic-church-conference-in-damascus/ [accessed 27/06/22].

493 "Patriarch: 'Christians in Lebanon will be extinct if West does nothing'", *ACN (US)*, 20th October 2021 https://www.churchinneed.org/patriarch-christians-will-be-extinct-if-west-does-nothing/ [accessed 27/06/22].

494 "Many Christians are short of hope…", *ACN (International)*, op. cit.

495 John Pontifex, John Newton and Murcadha O Flaherty, Persecuted and Forgotten? A Report on Christians oppressed for their Faith, 2017-19, *Executive Summary*, p.14 https://persecutedchristians.acninternational.org/main-findings/ [accessed 27/06/22].

496 Frances Martel, "Report: Syria lost over 60 percent of its Christians in a decade", *Breitbart*, 10th August 2021 https://www.breitbart.com/faith/2021/08/10/report-syria-lost-60-percent-its-christians-decade/ [accessed 27/06/22].

497 Karwan Faidhi Dri, "Syria's Christian population reduced by two-thirds since 2011: party", *RUDAW*, 9th August 2021 https://www.rudaw.net/english/middleeast/syria/090820211 [accessed 27/06/22].

498 "Syrian Christians: Life between war and migration", *Coptic Solidarity*, 13th June 2022 https://www.copticsolidarity.org/2022/06/13/syrian-christians-life-between-war-and-migration/ [accessed 29/06/22].

499 Jack Doyle, "Persecution of Christians is modern-day 'genocide' says report…", *Daily Mail*, 2nd May 2019 https://www.dailymail.co.uk/news/article-6986565/Persecution-Christians-modern-day-genocide-says-report.html [accessed 27/06/22].

500 "Patriarch: 'Christians in Lebanon will be extinct if West does nothing'", *ACN (US)*, 20th October 2021 https://www.churchinneed.org/patriarch-christians-will-be-extinct-if-west-does-nothing/ [accessed 27/06/22].

501 US State Dept., "Syria", *2020 Report on International Religious Freedom* https://www.state.gov/reports/2020-report-on-international-religious-freedom/syria/ [accessed 27/06/22].

502 Ibid.

503 USCIRF, "Syria", *2022*, op. cit., p. 35.

504 "Christians Left in Syria's Idlib Struggle Amid Banned Religious Practices And Property Seizure, *North Press Agency*, 5th March 2022 https://npasyria.com/en/73751/ [accessed 27/06/22].

505 Sirwan Kajjo, "Christians Concerned About Turkish Attacks in Northeast Syria", 14th September 2021, *VOA*, https://www.voanews.com/a/6227751.html [accessed 27/06/22].

506 John Pontifex, "Mothers and children scavenge for food in bins", *ACN (UK)*, 23rd July 2022 https://acnuk.org/news/syria-mothers-and-children-scavenge-for-food-in-bins/ [accessed 27/06/22].

507 "Millions Below Poverty Line, US Tightens Sanctions", *Syrian Observatory for Human Rights*, 28th June 2020 https://www.syriahr.com/en/172275/ [accessed 27/06/22].

508 "Syria's food shortage worsens as Covid-19 threatens to escalate", *TRT World*, 26th June 2020 https://www.trtworld.com/middle-east/syria-s-food-shortage-worsens-as-covid-19-threatens-to-escalate-37619 [accessed 27/06/22].

509 "Syria emergency", *UNHCR*, https://www.unhcr.org/syria-emergency.html [accessed 27/06/22].

510 Ibid.

511 US State Dept., "Syria", *2020 Report on International Religious Freedom*, https://www.state.gov/reports/2020-report-on-international-religious-freedom/syria/ [accessed 27/06/22].

512 Amberin Zaman, "Turkey's illegal renditions of Syrian nationals back in spotlight", *Al-Monitor*, 1st July 2021 https://www.al-monitor.com/originals/2021/07/turkeys-illegal-renditions-syrian-nationals-back-spotlight [accessed 27/06/22].

513 Sirwan Kajjo, "Christians Concerned About Turkish Attacks in Northeast Syria", *VOA*, 14th September 2021 https://www.voanews.com/a/6227751.html [accessed 27/06/22].

514 Ibid.

515 "Chaldean priest: Christians in Syria are in desperate need of help," *Vatican News*, 20th December 2021 https://www.vaticannews.va/en/church/news/2021-12/syria-christian-exodus-from-kurdish-controlled-jazira-region.html [accessed 27/06/22].

516 "International aid essential for Christians to survive in Syria", *Vatican News*, 3rd January 2021 https://www.vaticannews.va/en/church/news/2022-01/international-aid-essential-for-christians-to-survive-in-syria.html [accessed 27/06/22].

517 "Assyrian church destroyed by Turkish shelling in northeastern Syria", *Asianews*, 6th January 2022 https://www.Asianews.it/news-en/Assyrian-church-destroyed-by-Turkish-shelling-in-northeastern-Syria-55938.html [accessed 27/06/22].

518 "Syria's Christian Population Dwindles to Nearly Nothing", *International Christian Concern*, 6th February 2022 https://www.persecution.org/2022/02/06/syrias-christian-population-dwindles-nearly-nothing/ [accessed 27/06/22].

519 "Bishop Audo: Damascus conference is like Pentecost of the Syrian Church", *Asianews*, 17th March 2022 https://www.Asianews.it/news-en/Bishop-Audo%3A-Damascus-conference-is-like-Pentecost-of-the-Syrian-Church-55380.html [accessed 27/06/22].

520 "Many Christians are short of hope…", *ACN (International)*, op. cit.

521 Chiara Zappa, "Mar Musa monastery reopens, welcomes pilgrims and visitors again," *Asianews*, 21st June 2022 https://www.Asianews.it/news-en/Mar-Musa-monastery-reopens,-welcomes-pilgrims-and-visitors-again-56087.html [accessed 27/06/22].

522 "Bishop Nassar: young people, Church and families victims of Syrian war", *Asianews*, 9th June 2022 https://www.Asianews.it/news-en/Bishop-Nassar:-young-people,-Church-and-families-victims-of-Syrian-war-55993.html [accessed 27/06/22].

523 "Casualties reported after attack on church inauguration in Syria", *CNA*, 24th July 2022 https://www.catholicnewsagency.com/news/251867/attack-on-syrian-church-inauguration-kills-at-least-one [accessed 10/08/22].

524 "Turkish President Erdoğan recites Islamic prayer at the Hagia Sophia", *Hürriyet*, 1st April 2018 https://www.hurriyetdailynews.com/turkish-president-erdogan-recites-islamic-prayer-at-the-hagia-sophia-129594 ; "Hagia Sophia's status to be changed to mosque: Erdoğan", *Hürriyet*, 28th March 2019 https://www.hurriyetdailynews.com/hagia-sophias-status-to-be-changed-to-mosque-erdogan-142230 [both sites accessed 24/05/22].

525 "Ecumenical Patriarch Bartholomew about Hagia Sophia", *Ecumenical Patriarchate Permanent Delegation to the World Council of Churches*, 30th June 2020 https://www.ecupatria.org/2020/06/30/ecumenical-patriarch-bartholomew-about-hagia-sophia/ [accessed 24/05/22].

526 "Frescoes in İstanbul's Chora Museum covered up ahead of first Friday prayer", *BIA News*, 28th October 2020 https://m.bianet.org/english/religion/233487-frescoes-in-istanbul-s-chora-museum-covered-up-ahead-of-first-friday-prayer [accessed 24/05/22].

527 "Has Turkey halted plans to turn Chora museum into a mosque?", *Art Newspaper*, 11th January 2021 https://www.theartnewspaper.com/2021/01/11/has-turkey-halted-plans-to-turn-chora-museum-into-a-mosque [accessed 24/05/22].

528 "UNESCO criticizes Ankara over conversion of Hagia Sophia, Chora Monastery", *e-Kathimerini*, 23rd July 2011 https://www.ekathimerini.com/news/1165097/unesco-criticises-ankara-about-conversion-of-hagia-sophia-chora-monastery/ [accessed 24/05/22].

529 "50th Anniversary of the Closing of Halki Seminary", *USCIRF*, 29th July 2021 https://www.state.gov/50th-anniversary-of-the-closing-of-halki-seminary/ ; "Tanju Bilgiç'ten Ned Price'a 'Heybeliada Ruhban Okulu' cevabı", *Dünya Bülteni*, 29th July 2021 https://www.dunyabulteni.net/dis-politika/tanju-bilgic-ten-ned-price-a-heybeliada-ruhban-okulu-h506205.html [both sites accessed 24/05/22].

530 "Assyrian Church Attacked and Desecrated in Eastern Turkey", *AINA*, 14th May 2021 http://www.aina.org/news/20210514182659.htm [accessed 18/05/22]; "Kidnapped parents of well-known Chaldean Catholic priest still missing after a month", *Premier Christian News*, 12th February 2020 https://premierchristian.news/en/news/article/kidnapped-parents-of-well-known-chaldean-catholic-priest-still-missing-after-a-month [accessed 19/05/22]. It is believed that Hormoz Diril is the same man who was jailed in Beytussebab prison in 1994, after enquiring about the detention of his brothers, Zeki Ercan Diril and Ilyas Edip Diril by state security forces. Kovankaya, the Chaldean village